SOMETHING IS BETTER THAN NOTHING

ALICIA DELORY

D1316906

"I dare you to open Alicia Delory's 'Something is Better than Nothing' and then try to put it down. This is a page-turning narrative that exposes physical and emotional shrapnel, relayed with unflinching and poetic honesty. Through her woven reflection on loving a veteran and mourning the loss of her father, Delory attains a rare and sharp beauty, laced with humor and hard-won wisdom."

— SONYA HUBER, AUTHOR OF PAIN
WOMAN TAKES YOUR KEYS

This stunning memoir relates a rarely heard account of a wife surviving her army husband's return from Afghanistan with severe PTSD. Their story of perseverance, anger, violence, and a yearning for understanding, are interspersed with gripping scenes from Delory's difficult childhood. Told with searing frankness, dark humor, and penetrating insight, here is a riveting true story of how fierce honesty and enduring love can heal immeasurable challenges.

— EUGENIA KIM, AUTHOR OF THE
KINSHIP OF SECRETS

ISBN (pbk) 978-1-947041-76-9

ISBN (ebook) 978-1-947041-77-6

Published in North America and Europe by Running Wild Press. Visit Running
Wild Press at www.runningwildpress.com Educators, librarians, book clubs (as
well as the eternally curious), go to www.runningwildpress.com.

For Mom and Dad

HOMECOMING

M y husband didn't return home in a flag-draped silver casket. No uniformed men came to my door telling me that he wasn't coming home. He wasn't immortalized with a patriotic motorcade or a three-volley salute. No member of an Honor Guard presented me with a 13-fold American flag. Specialist (SPC) Barksdale wasn't listed among the Killed, Wounded, or Missing in Action soldiers of Operation Enduring Freedom. And because none of these things happened, I flipped through the pages of my calendar and traced a heart around March 22, 2012 with the word "Chris" scribbled in the middle. I thought my days spent alone and waiting had come to an end; I didn't know then that they had barely begun. I was about to learn the true meaning of loneliness.

SPC Barksdale arrives in Germany, worn and weary, on his own two feet, marching into the gymnasium that's crudely decorated with handmade poster board signs, after standing outside for nearly an hour in the freezing cold because some of the wives were running late for the homecoming ceremony. A fog machine, meant to create a dramatic effect — because nothing lacks drama like a bunch of men returning home from war — fills the gym with thick fog that leaves the attendees choking on its showmanship. The happy sobs and cheers of the family members of his platoon blare and echo off the walls as the soldiers enter the foggy gymnasium. It's a cruel way to welcome someone home from war, but I don't know that yet. I'm too wrapped up in my own jubilation to notice much else, so I stand tall in the bleachers, screaming and holding up my poorly drawn, "WELCOME HOME SPC BARKSDALE!" sign, ugly crying, and scanning the crowd for my husband.

I was the first one here. I got the call that they were wheels up, and I grabbed the sign I'd made and ran out the door to collect my man. I'd spent the evening primping, picking out the right outfit, and Nairing parts of my body that hadn't seen a razor since Chris had come home for R & R seven months before. Our apartment is clean from top to bottom. I have a fridge full of food and snacks warming in the crockpot. They told us at the Family Readiness Group (FRG) meetings not to introduce too much change too fast, as reintegration is a delicate process. I decided that small changes were permissible – an accent table here, new curtains there, a French Bulldog puppy, and a newly blonde, 70-pounds-lighter wife, but otherwise, everything would be exactly as he left it.

We'd arrived in Ansbach, Germany two years before. He was fresh out of basic training, and I'd just finished my bachelor's degree. I'd also just warmed to the idea of picking up my entire life to follow him wherever his career took him. Six months before I joined him in Germany, we were living with his father and stepmother in Eden, Georgia. Chris had just told me he wanted to join the Army, and I was throwing my engagement ring at his head. We were supposed to have a long engagement. I was supposed to go on to grad school. He was supposed to save up money and go to nursing school.

"So, you just up and decide to enlist and I'm supposed to drop everything and follow you around?"

"I've been thinking about this for a while —"

"Fuck you," I screamed as my white-gold and half-carat engagement ring bounced off his neck. I pulled my empty suitcase from the top of the closet and began throwing in whatever I could. He left to join his father in their living room.

I don't know how I came around, or even the conversation that followed. I just remember that one minute, he was leaving me in the bedroom to angrily pack my suitcase, and the next I was sitting on the bed with him, saying, "Okay, tell me what you have in mind," while he sold me on his plan to pay off his debts and create a stable life for us and suddenly, we were planning to get married four weeks later – more than two years earlier than we'd planned. We convinced ourselves that it made sense; after all, we were already engaged. I could get on his medical insurance. We could have a home of our own instead of bouncing between my college dorm and his father's house. We wouldn't have to be in a long-distance relationship for the next two years, waiting until the Army allowed him some time off to marry me. It *did* make sense; that's what we told ourselves. In reality, we were twenty-two, and we knew our engagement wouldn't survive if he left. I knew getting married that young was a bad idea, but I wasn't ready to be without him.

I loved him. Love was a good enough reason. It *had* to be.

I remember him talking to me on our wedding day as we took photos on his father's back porch, telling me how different our lives would be – how we wouldn't be stuck with a shitty car anymore, like the $500 beat-up Honda Civic that you could hear from a mile away, held together mostly by duct tape. It was a manual, and I couldn't drive it, despite Chris trying on four separate occasions to teach me how to use a stick shift.

"Baby, someday we'll be able to afford fancy things, like an iron," he said, completely straight-faced, and certain that his enlistment would make our lives better; we just had to get through the next few months. We'd be married and, less than twenty-four hours later, he'd be leaving for basic training. As a joke, my mother-in-law gave us an iron as a wedding gift.

"See? Things are already looking up," he said.

So, for his homecoming, I figured he'd be happy to see how the fruits of his labor paid off, because if there's one thing soldiers worry about during wartime, it's being able to afford home décor and cute puppies for their newly slim wives.

I spend my time frantically searching the small group of maybe forty soldiers for Chris's face, with little luck. Later, when I view the photographs that fellow onlookers snapped that day, I'll see Chris standing in formation, his eyes fixed forward, staring at nothing and everything, while some officer who probably doesn't know his name, and who's spent a year sitting behind a desk and a pile of paperwork, welcomes him home, and reminds the crowd that they are in the company of American heroes.

"Where is he? I don't see him. Why can't I see him?" I whisper to my friend, Taryn, who's accompanied me this morning to take pictures, and who only knows Chris from the pictures I've shown her at work. He has sandy brown hair and big blue eyes and the longest eyelashes I've ever seen on a man. He isn't a tall guy, but I forgive that because of his stocky build, broad shoulders, and his effortless six pack; I affectionately refer to him as my pocket-sized Rambo. He has a permanent, beautiful set of dimples. When he walks, he has a literal pep in his step due in part to short Achilles tendons and in part to his chronically cheerful demeanor.

In the months, weeks, and days leading up to his deployment, I'd look at him, trying to memorize everything about him.

That face that always put me at ease.

His voice, he almost never raised, with its soft, subtle Georgia dialect that always sounded like home.

The kindness of his eyes, and the way they always seemed to smile when he talked or whenever he looked at me.

The way his dimples always stayed intact, even when he was upset or sad, acting like little beacons of hope, always reassuring me and everyone around him that all would be well. I loved that the most.

"Promise you'll stay you?" I'd urge him, and he'd smile at me and promise, "Of course, Sweetie. I'm not going anywhere."

"Promise you'll come home?"

"Of course, Sweetie." We repeated this exchange like a mantra while I held him and said goodbye to him in the parking lot behind the barracks the night he left, like if we said it enough, it would be etched into whatever cosmic plan was laid out for the next twelve months, and he would come home just fine, alive, and in one piece, whatever the hell I thought that meant.

While he was in Afghanistan, we would video chat a few times a month, sometimes less. His voice got deeper and hoarser as his deployment wore on. So, each time we talked and I asked, "You still you?" his response of, "I'm still me," grew more and more mechanical, and less and less convincing.

After a short speech, the soldiers are dismissed and a stampede of happy family members rushes into the dispersing formation of green. Another sadistic gesture in our unrelenting effort to welcome home a group of men and women who've spent the last year of their lives in a permanent state of hyper-vigilance.

"There! Right there!" Taryn points at a man, about Chris's height, but who looks a bit older, not in a wrinkly and gray type of way, but in the way that cracks in pavement give away the weight of its many burdens.

I bee-line toward the man who looks vaguely like an older, exhausted version of my husband, my arms outstretched and my face contorted from tears of joy and relief. When he sees me, his face remains tired, and he uses what little energy he has to raise his arms slightly away from his sides. I grab him and hold him tight, as I cry into his neck and shoulder, no doubt leaving a trail of tears and snot behind, another fine way to receive a soldier back into his civilian life.

"You're here. You're *here*. I'm sorry I'm boogering all over you. You're here!"

He pushes my face away so my eyes meet his. "I'm here. Why are you crying? I'm here," he says, not comforting me, but urging me to get a hold of myself.

This reaffirmation of his presence makes my crying louder and more dramatic, and I bury my face back into his uniform and sob some more, until finally some older woman I don't know hands me a tissue and smiles at me with tears in her eyes.

A photographer is capturing vignettes of each family's reunion. A few months from now, a photo of our embrace will be blown up and plastered outside the new Post Exchange, and at first, I'll love it and I'll feel special that *our* picture is on display for all to see. My love for it will fade, though, and eventually, I'll cringe every time I see it. When we move back to Georgia, I'll be relieved, because I won't have to stare at the fucking picture of those two strangers any more.

We step off to the side to pose for photos, SPC Barksdale mustering up his best version of a smile, and our poses looking like an awkward, middle school dance portrait. I will love these pictures at first, the way I loved the PX photo. I'm so blissfully, obliviously relieved and happy because my prayers for him to come home alive have been answered. There are different kinds of survival, but I don't know that yet either.

In the months that follow, I'll find him sitting around the house, staring into space, like his brain is a skipping CD. I'll get used to him scanning other cars when we drive anywhere, and looking around for anything resembling a threat as we walk hand-in-hand through the mall.

His mind will always be somewhere else, rarely with me or our life together. I'll see him on alert all day long and wonder what he is bracing himself for, but I know that asking will only make him angry and feel even more alienated. Each incident will drop another hint that the Chris I knew never came back, and wherever he is now, he exists in some limbo somewhere between there and here.

They trained me to be there. Nobody taught me how to be here.

From time to time, I'll picture him back in that gymnasium, bombarded by a hero's welcome, looking more exhausted than anyone I'd ever seen, as the crowd disperses to partake in coffee and pastries and friendly hellos. My soldier who's returned to me safely, just as he'd promised, grabs my hand and pleads, "Let's just get my stuff off the bus and go home. I just want to go home." I don't see the desperation on his face as clearly as I will later on. His voice will play in my head through every episode, every panic attack, every time he scans a crowd: *I just want to go home.*

2

HOW WE MET

I waited by my window for my date to show up. I was twenty and I'd only been on two other dates: one with a guy I had no interest in, although I did want a free meal, and the other with a fireman I met on Match.com who photographed far better-looking than he actually was, and who spent half our date holding up the Jessica Simpson photo that was his cell phone background, shaking his head and saying, "Mmm. Dang. Woo wee!" He wasn't worth the free meal.

I had only a vague idea about what my date looked like. I had met him when I was drunk at some Halloween party the weekend before. I remember not wanting to go to another party. I'd been at a party every day for over a week, it was November 3rd, and Halloween was over already, dammit.

"Do I have to go? I feel like I've been drunk for a week," I moaned to my friend, Reuben, while I put mascara on.

"Yes. I'm not going alone."

"Whose party is this anyway?"

"Friend of a friend. His roommate is having a birthday party."

"Okay, but no guys."

"What happened with What's-His-Face?"

"He stayed over on Halloween and got back together with his girlfriend the next day."

"Ouch."

"Fuck guys."

"Don't mind if I do."

"You can have them. I'm done for now."

I left my apartment wearing fishnets, shorts that were actually bathing-suit bottoms, knee-high boots, a corset with a button-up shirt knotted just below my boobs, and a black leather cowboy hat that my mother's second husband had given me. I'd worn it everywhere when I first moved to Georgia from Massachusetts, but then I buried it in the back of my closet out of sheer humiliation when I realized that Southerners did not walk around in cowboy hats or address each other with, "Howdy."

Reuben, dressed as a shirtless Egyptian pharaoh, escorted me into the party. A pasty, blond guy dressed as a cop in blue shorts greeted us.

"This is his apartment. It's his birthday party," Reuben shouted over the music.

"Oh, cool. Happy Birthday. Where's the keg?"

As was customary for me at a party, I found the keg first. My friends always joked that I could sniff out booze from a mile away. "It's in my blood," I'd say, and as I got tipsy, I'd remind everyone, "I'm not drunk; I'm a Delory," because it's not sad if you're proud of it.

I filled up a plastic red cup to the brim, and chugged the whole beer. The trick was to open my throat and pour the beer into my mouth, slowly and steadily; that's how Dad did it. Slow is smooth and smooth is fast. I filled my cup again and found a spot on the patio to smoke. That was my M.O. at any party: Find the booze. Find a place to stand and smoke all night.

Reuben and I stood out on the patio, chain-smoking Parliaments. The air was humid, the night was just a little warmer than usual for November in South Georgia. Reuben made small talk with the people around us, introducing me to anyone he thought might entertain me. I stood behind him, smoking and pounding beers. As Reuben socialized and I drank and smoked and people-watched, a tall, balding kid with a goatee, who looked much older than he was, walked onto the patio with a touch-light under his red shirt – a piss-poor attempt at a Tony Stark costume. Behind him was a shorter guy wearing a long black wig, fuzzy red pants, and a matching red tube top. He looked like *Dirrty*-era Christina Aguilera. His nails were painted to match his outfit, and his eye makeup was smoky and sultry, and I could tell that someone who knew what they were doing had helped him with it.

Tony Stark and Christina made their way to the sparsely crowded patio, smiling with their unlit Kools in hand.

"Is there any room out here?" Christina asked jokingly, with a grin from ear to ear.

"No," I answered flatly as I returned to my conversation with Reuben.

Christina, not understanding sarcasm, turned to Tony, genuinely hurt and indignant.

"What the hell's *her* problem?"

I spent most of the night on the patio, only leaving to refill my plastic cup. The party became more and more crowded. My friend Sally showed up dressed as Lady Liberty. Heather showed up in metallic body paint, dressed as a robot. Some girl named Kristie was always nearby, dressed as a Black Widow spider. After an hour or two, the night devolved into seeing who would make out with whom, and I was drunk enough to play along.

"No guys," I said, wagging my finger at our circle of friends, both old and new.

"I'm not a guy!" Sally shouted as we locked lips and the crowd cheered.

"Me, too!" Kristie shouted, as she joined in, and we, drunkenly, and probably sloppily, made out with each other. The cheers from the party grew louder and we kissed longer.

We finally parted, and the crowd clapped and cheered as we scrambled to find something else to entertain ourselves. Kristie grabbed Christina, who'd been lurking around our circle and cheering along with the rest of the party-goers.

"What about him?"

"I'm off dudes right now," I grumbled as I finished my beer.

"Yeah, but he's not a boy," Kristie laughed.

"Yeah, I'm a girl!" Christina shouted, still smiling.

"Oh, okay," I conceded, as I grabbed them both by the back of their heads and they stuck their tongues in my mouth. Christina's friends roared as we triple-kissed.

"That was awesome," Christina squealed, unable to keep his cool about kissing two girls at once.

"I need another beer," I muttered as I went back to the keg.

Heather started to have an allergic reaction to her metallic body paint, and was showering in the bathroom that all the guests were using. I stood in line, waiting for the toilet. When it was my turn, I opened the door and sat down on the toilet.

"Hey, Heather."

"Hey! Who's there?"

"It's Alicia."

"Oh, hi. Did I see you making out with Christina?"

"Yeah. And Sally. And Kristie."

"Nice. This paint will not come off."

She kept talking as I noticed her Marlboro Lights on the back of the toilet. My Parliaments were running low. I took a few and shoved them in my corset.

"Bye, Heather. See you out there."

Heather finally finished her shower and walked around the party for the rest of the night, wrapped in a towel. Right before the police came, we went to the porch where the keg was, talking and laughing.

"I need to go to the bathroom," she said.

"Get in line," I said, pointing at the line down the hallway.

"I can't wait."

"Go in the woods."

"I'll just go here," she said, as she spread her legs near the slats of the second-floor porch.

"No way. You can't aim that. You'll make a mess," I said, as I watched in fascination as she managed to pee off the side of the porch with nary a sprinkle.

"Heather, that was fucking amazing," I said, taking another gulp from my beer.

"I have to poop," she said, laughing and turning around so her ass faced the slats.

"No way," I said, horrified, but fascinated.

I heard people laughing and shouting from the living room. "Dude, that chick's shitting off the porch," someone said, pointing at the girl in the towel who was somehow shitting off the side of the porch and defying all the rules of physics and gravity.

"Shit. Cops!" someone screamed. I finished what was left of my beer, found Reuben, and hauled ass for the door. As we made our way through the crowd, I heard some guy talking about Christina. "Dude, I thought that was a chick. Holy shit." We ran through the parking lot, and a car stopped in front of us and its rear window rolled down.

"Get in," someone shouted. Reuben pushed me in the car and sat next to me. They took us to a nearby apartment, where we were to hide. It occurred to me that I didn't know who these people were, and I started to pray that Reuben did.

"Alicia, this is Myr," Reuben said as a skinny blonde kid waved to me. *Thank God. That could've been bad.* I silently promised to the powers-that-be that if I could make it through this night without getting arrested or murdered, I'd make better decisions from there on out.

For some reason I don't remember — probably beer — we waited a while, but went back to the party. When we arrived, there were ten or fifteen people hanging out. I went to the back porch where the keg was, and Christina was sitting in a folding chair, sipping beer. I picked up the first empty cup I could find and I walked past him to fill it.

"Hi," he said, smiling.

"Hi. This is getting low," I said as I shook the all-but-floated keg. Then I asked, "Why'd you dress like Christina Aguilera?"

"I'm not Christina Aguilera. Why does everyone think that?"

"Because you look like Christina Aguilera," I said, gulping down my beer, trying to regain the buzz that had been harshed by the police showing up.

"Anyway, I'm just a girl. No girl in particular."

"Why'd you dress like a girl?"

"I couldn't think of anything else."

"That's a stupid reason," I said, rolling my eyes and sipping my beer. I walked over to him and put my hand on his smooth chest.

"Did you shave your chest?"

"Yeah, and my stomach," he said, smiling.

I grabbed his pecs.

"Why didn't you give yourself boobs?"

"I didn't think I needed them."

I put his hand on my boob.

"*This* is a boob. Now feel yours. Not realistic," I said, smiling, fluttering my eyelashes, still drinking. Truth be told, his constant grinning annoyed me. It reminded me of this kid named Andrew that was in my kindergarten class. He was always sitting next to me, smiling for no reason. One day, I punched him as hard as I could. My teacher sent a note home to my parents. I wanted to punch Christina. But it was the end of the night, and I also wanted to get laid.

He wrapped his arms around my waist, and we started swaying on the porch, but there was no music. I clutched my cup, finishing the last gulp, and I put my free hand on his lower back. I felt a curly patch of hair.

"Why would you shave your chest and your stomach, but not your back?"

"Oops," he said, pulling me closer to him and grinning.

"The keg's empty," someone shouted. Since I always prioritized alcohol over sex, I pulled myself from Christina's grasp and left, never meaning to see him again. After all, what kind of a woman meets her husband in the middle of a drunken triple-kiss with another girl while he's dressed in drag for Halloween?

This is what I asked myself as Christina's white Tacoma pickup truck pulled into my parking lot later the next week. A few days after the party, he managed to find me and send me a friend request on social media. It turned out that his name was Chris and he (supposedly) didn't always party or drink like that.

"Yeah, me either," I had lied.

And then, when he finally asked me out, I paused to call my mother.

"Mom, some tranny I met at a Halloween party last weekend just asked me out."

"Is he cute?"

"I don't know. I've never seen him as a guy," I said.

"Oh, just take a chance, Alicia."

I decided to take the advice of my mother, who was in the midst of her second divorce and was very much enjoying her newfound freedom as a single woman in Atlanta's middle-aged dating scene. She'd also just started corresponding with some guy from the Midwest she'd met in an online chatroom who would eventually become her third husband.

I looked down from my window, and held my breath as a shorter, muscular guy stepped out of the driver's side door. He had sandy brown hair and he wore jeans and a blue-and-white, striped polo shirt. He had a puka shell necklace, which I forgave because even from my second-story window, I could see his dimples and his gorgeous blue eyes. I met him at my door and he looked down at my shoes, a bright orange pair of Kangaroos.

"Sweet Roos," he said.

Someone *might* meet her husband this way. Either way, it was one hell of a story.

3
HOW THEY MET

I'd been told by both of my parents, even long after they'd been divorced, that theirs was a romantic story. In 1985, they were working together at a Dunkin Donuts, situated just behind T.F. Green Airport in Warwick, which is the second largest city in Rhode Island. In fact, travelers flying into Providence were actually landing in Warwick. The roar of planes taking off and landing could be heard all day long, but residents were so used to it that nobody ever noticed.

One of Mom and Dad's regular customers, Jimmy, was sitting at the counter one day, back when customer interaction still trumped turnover at coffee and donut shops. Patrons could enjoy a hot cup of coffee, perched on barstools and talking with each other, instead of barking their orders into some perforated box outside.

My mother and father were in the kitchen in the back and, as usual, my father's wise cracks and cocky remarks — which were meant as flirtation — had pushed my mother over the edge. Jimmy sipped his black coffee as the café walls reverberated from the clang of muffin pans being hurled across the kitchen, narrowly missing my father's head. Jimmy kept sipping his hot coffee as my mother stormed through the swinging kitchen doors and my father followed close behind, smirking.

"You're a fucking prick," she said through clenched teeth.

"Oh, come on. I was just kidding," he laughed.

"Fuck you." She grabbed a wet rag and went about cleaning the café tables.

My father noticed Jimmy out of the corner of his eye.

"I see you two are getting along," Jimmy said.

My father held up his hands and shrugged, turning to go back into the kitchen.

"Hey, Ray," Jimmy began, as my father turned back to him, "You're gonna marry that girl."

Romantic.

* * *

Dad was seventeen and had a girlfriend whose name nobody seems to remember, which is odd because they'd had a baby together, a stillborn named Raymond that nobody ever talked about. Little Raymond was a baby that I only knew about because I'd overheard one of my Dad's trashy girlfriends talking about it when I was twelve, and because Dad always moaned, "I never got to know him," whenever he got especially wasted and melancholy. I've asked about him, but nobody seemed to agree about baby Raymond. All I know is that there was a baby boy who came from some chick that my dad dated before my mom, and the baby was either stillborn, or he lived for a few hours, or days, and then he died, and my father was sad about it and cried about it until the day *he* died. According to Mom, my grandmother made my father take photos with him holding the dead baby.

Nevertheless, Dad was dating the mother of his first child,

and Mom was engaged to some guy — I think his name was Michael — who apparently became a raging alcoholic later in life, which somehow made my mother feel better about leaving him to be with my father, though I'm not sure what made my drunk father better than some other drunk guy.

Mom was eighteen and a high school dropout when she met my father. She was the second child of five, and while her older brother was off tripping on acid and falsifying a high school diploma to get into college, she was raising one of my uncles and both of my aunts. Mom reminded me of that all the time. "I've been raising kids my whole life," she often said, and I felt bad that I'd added to her life sentence of taking care of everyone else. Mom was always thinking of everyone else. She told me that all the time, too.

My grandmother, Thelma, disciplined with her fists, and turned a blind eye to what my grandfather did to my mother and two aunts. She was often absent, taking off for days, weeks, or months at a time. It was unclear which bothered my mother more – the abuse or the abandonment. Sometimes, Thelma would dump her children off on the side of the road, and maybe that's how they ended up in foster care. I was about six the first time I heard that story, and as my younger sister and I lay on a single mattress on our bedroom floor — our bunk beds had been repossessed — we were reminded of how good we had it. We might not have beds, but at least our mother didn't hit us or leave us by the side of the road.

Dad was the second of four sons, and the first of his father's biological sons, a fact that his older brother, Stephen, never let him forget. When my grandfather and my grandmother, Larrain, divorced, she turned into a woman scorned, and my dad, the spitting image and namesake of her ex-husband, worked just fine as her punching bag.

Larrain was the kind of woman who called Big Ray and

told him that his boys were too sick for a visit, while those sons sat out on the front stoop, waiting for their father to arrive. That was always the story Dad told when he was feeling really sad and wasted, "I was just sitting there, waiting for my Dad to come pick me up," he slurred, "but he never did. I'd never do that to you girls." We hugged him. "We know, Daddy," we said, hugging and kissing him, understanding that a drunk dad was better than no dad at all.

Big Ray eventually distanced himself, in the hopes that his sons would be spared the torture of Larrain's wrath should they continue to love him. Despite Big Ray's best intentions, the boys were disciplined with two-by-fours and reminded constantly that they were nothing, just like their father. My father bore the brunt of her cruelty, and doing it without his father made it worse, and made him angrier. Dad latched onto his mother, become more soldier than son, and believed every word she said. If Larrain told him he was nothing, then that's what he was, and that's what he would always be. By the time he met my mother, he'd picked up a smoking and drinking habit and was, in many ways, still a kid just sitting on the front steps, waiting for his father to arrive.

So, there they were, a woman who'd spent her life taking care of everyone else, and a man who desperately needed to be taken care of, arguing and throwing pans at each other in the back kitchen of Dunkin Donuts. It's no wonder they found each other.

My mother began softening toward my father after his girl-friend broke up with him. He started showing up to work, quiet and morose, not uttering one cocky remark or snarky comment. "He was just so sad," Mom tells me, and I know what she means; Dad's brooding had a way of commanding attention. It was deep and over-the-top and contagious. When Dad's heart broke, so did everyone else's. His sulking was exhausting and impossible to ignore; it just weighed down the air in the room until finally, with no other options, someone broke down and asked him what was the matter. It's no wonder she approached him to try and help; I'd have taken pissed-off-running-his-mouth Dad over sad Dad any day.

Mom lent Dad a shoulder to cry on as she reached out and asked him what was wrong. He didn't deflect with a witty retort, but poured his heart out about his break-up and how he didn't think his girlfriend would ever take him back.

"Buy her some flowers, tell her you're sorry, and everything will be fine," Mom told him in their first interaction that didn't involve cheap shots or flying bakeware.

Eventually, after the screaming matches and physical altercations slowed down, my parents established a rapport and a friendship. One day, Dad asked Mom out on a date.

"I'm bringing my brother," he said.

"Well if *you're* bringing someone, then I'm bringing someone, too."

In the photographs from that night, it was New Year's Eve. Mom, Dad, Uncle David, and Kim Razza, my future godmother, were lined up in front of a limousine my father had rented; my mother and Kim were holding flowers that Dad and Uncle had brought them. Kim and David were there to keep Dad from feeling too nervous. It didn't look awkward the way most first dates do, with the painful silences, useless small talk, hives, nervous farting, and that klutzy dance at the end where you try and figure out whether to go in for a hug, or a kiss, or handshake. Maybe that was just how my first dates played out.

Or maybe that was the whole point of Dad bringing someone with him, so he could avoid all of that. Mom and Dad looked happy and affectionate and familiar in a way that made it seem like they'd been together for a long time. In those photographs, they hugged and nuzzled. Mom wore a silky, fuchsia blouse with a bow on the neck, and she fooled around with a black fedora that someone had brought along. Dad, wearing a white button-up and tan pants that were way too tight, leaned on her shoulder with his eyes closed and grinned from ear to ear.

Six weeks later, my father proposed, and they were married in June. The following New Year's Eve, they had me, on purpose. Two teenagers from broken homes, one an alcoholic, both of them high school drop-outs, found each other, started throwing pans at each other, but then fell in love, and got married and had babies. And then they got divorced some years later because two adults from broken homes, one an alcoholic, kept throwing shit at each other, and fell out of love because it's a bad idea to get married and have babies when you're two teenage high school drop-outs from broken homes.

It was a romantic story – one where love was the blurry line between romance and red flag. Love, just like everything else in our lives, was supposed to be hard.

4

BOWLING

Chris got home two days ago. It's been sunny and warm, which is odd for Germany in March. But we haven't been out much. Normally, we'd be outside, rejoicing in the fact that "BOB's out!" BOB was the sun and stood for "Big Orange Blob," and the custom among all of us on the military post was to get excited about BOB because he almost never came out until the end of spring. But that was before, and now we're in the after, and Chris doesn't give a shit about BOB, or anything else.

We've been invited to go bowling with some of his battle buddies, and I've emphatically accepted the invitation for the both of us. He's spent the last two days sleeping, refusing to eat my cooking because its smell reminds him of some Shepherd's Pie he threw up downrange, and fucking me like he's trying to get back at someone. He spends a lot of time lying on the couch with our new puppy, not saying much. I'm glad he has the puppy; a part of me wonders if he loves her so much because she didn't know him before. I'll be glad to see him interacting with other soldiers. It's only been two days, but it's already apparent that he doesn't have anything to say to me.

A big, burly guy named Hatcher – who will go on to marry my sister some years later – greets me as we find our lane. A smaller, thinner guy named Wolfe waves hello, and some other soldiers I can't remember introduce themselves.

"How are you, Hatcher?" I ask him as I scan his face for anything familiar. Instead, he looks down, just like he did when I saw him in the parking lot on Thursday.

"I'm good," he lies, "Happy to be out of that shithole."

"I'll bet." The group falls silent as everyone either puts on their bowling shoes or looks down at their phones. I know not to ask him anything else. I put my hand on Chris's back and lean down to his ear. "I'll get us some drinks," I say as I leave for the concession stand.

Don't ask too many questions. Don't feel sorry for them. Don't look at them like you feel bad for them. Don't tell them how happy you are to have them back.

"I'll take two Coronas, please," I say to the cashier.

"No, wait. I'll take a bucket." The cashier raises an eyebrow and smiles at me as he rings me up and hands me a six pack of open bottles of beer. He looks at me the way I'd look at Dad when he'd ask me to bring him cans of Coors two at a time. Dad would read my mind and say, "Don't be a smartass," and I'd silently bring him his beers and realize that he was way smarter than any of us gave him credit for.

I take my time walking back to the lane and start drinking from one of the bottles.

Don't ask questions. Smile, but not too much.

When I arrive at our lane, the game has already started.

"You're up," Chris says as he takes a beer and turns away from me to talk to Wolfe. As I begin bowling my first frame, I realize that I am the only spouse there. I feel out of place and a little special.

Just keep quiet. Fetch the beers and food. Be the cool wife. Blend in.

I sit down after my turn and reach for my second beer while everyone around me chats and bowls. Hatcher sees that I'm sitting alone and makes his way over to me.

"Is it good to have him home?" he asks.

He doesn't talk to me much or really look at me, and he stares into space while he angry fucks me.

"Very."

"You keeping him in line?"

"Always."

"Told you I'd make sure we got back," he laughs.

You sure did.

"Good job, Hatcher," I say as I pat him on the back. Everyone gathers together and it's time for a smoke break. I sit back and wait to see if I'm invited.

"You coming?" Chris looks at me and I get up and follow the crowd outside. They're beginning to include me more, and more familiar faces are trickling into the bowling alley, hugging me on their way in, telling me how great I look, and asking "Aren't you so happy to have him home?"

The crowd disperses and now it's just Chris, Hatcher, Wolfe, and myself. They start talking about Afghanistan and how Sergeant or Lieutenant So-and-So lost their shit about how someone didn't clean up something well enough.

"Yeah, I heard there were still pieces of them left in the vehicle," Chris says.

"He screwed the pooch on that one," Hatcher says.

"What?" I ask.

Dumbass. Don't ask questions.

"You remember the three guys we lost? That vehicle," Chris explains.

"I was really good friends with Schumann," Hatcher says.

I decide to leave them to their discussion. I wouldn't understand. They keep talking and I go back inside to the concession stand.

"Another bucket, please. Coronas."

"Back already?" the cashier asks.

Don't be a smartass. I point to the guys outside still talking.

"I'm with that group." I drank four beers out of the six-pack, but he doesn't need to know that.

The guys come back from smoking and we continue our game. They talk to each other, but only about things that I've already been told by my husband that I wouldn't understand or care to hear about, so I keep quiet and bowl my frames.

"She made this fucking dip and it smelled just like that Shepherd's Pie," Chris says.

"I know you didn't eat that," Hatcher says.

"Fuck, no. Remember? We were all throwing it up and shitting ourselves?"

"That was rough, man."

My bad, asshole.

"I'd probably still eat it," Hatcher says to me.

"Good. You can have it," Chris says.

"That's fucked up, man. She made you a nice meal. Are you going to let this guy diss your cooking like that?" Hatcher says, waiting for me to shoot my husband my famous glare that always made everyone fall in line. I smile back at him and shrug. My husband never used to talk shit about me. He used to brag about me, tell anyone who would listen that I had a degree, even if it was just an English degree that wasn't worth the paper it was printed on. "She's gonna write a book someday," he'd say. He was good like that, always seeing good things about me, even if I couldn't see them in myself. He never used to insult me in private, never mind in public. Then again, I never used to shrink back and take it. That was before. People are different in the after.

After three games and four buckets of beer, we call it a night. Chris and I decide to walk home to our apartment and leave our car in the parking lot until the morning. As we say goodbye, Chris takes me by the hand. He always held my hand before, but now he clenches it the way my Mom used to when I was a kid and I'd just gotten in trouble. He pulls my arm when he does it, because since he's gotten home, he walks everywhere like he's in a hurry. We walk the first few minutes hand-in-hand as I hold a box of leftover pizza and he drags me down the street, until finally he gets tired of pleasantries and starts walking about ten feet ahead of me.

"That was fun," he says, his back still turned to me.

"Yeah. It was good to see Hatcher."

"Yeah."

"I still think he and Amanda would be perfect for each other."

"Me, too."

This is something we always talked about before we left. We always tried to play matchmaker between Hatcher and my sister, saying that we like him so much that we want him to be our brother. It's nice to revisit the conversation. For a second, it's nice to be the people we were before Afghanistan.

We stumble in the door, and he does the usual climbing on top of me and grunting while he stares at the wall or looks through me, but I'm too drunk to be annoyed by it. I don't need much eye contact, in fact, it used to freak me out when he looked at me too much or if he said, "I love you," during. But he doesn't do any of that anymore, which felt sexy and carnal at first, but now it's just downright lonely and degrading.

When he's done, I go into the kitchen and grab the box of pizza off the counter and bring it back into the bedroom.

"Oh, good idea," he says, flinging the lid open. For a brief moment, we're us again.

"I know, right?" I say as I begin to giggle.

"What's so funny?" he asks, smiling with his mouth full of pizza. I can't say anything because I'm giggling too hard, as is customary for me after a few drinks.

"What's so funny?" He asks again, this time, no smile.

Post-coital pizza in bed. It's funny, dumbass.

I throw my head back, laughing even harder, still struggling to get the words out, and completely oblivious to his growing agitation. He throws his slice down into the box and grabs the hair at the nape of my neck, jerking my head back so that my eyes meet his.

"I said, what's so funny?" he bellows, his wide, bloodshot eyes piercing through me.

I scream, and he releases his grip and raises his hands up, signaling that he's no threat to me. I clasp both of my hands over my mouth and turn my back to him. If the neighbors hear, they'll call the MPs and Chris could get in trouble for a domestic incident.

I freeze, my hands still over my mouth, as if staying still will make me invisible.

"What was so funny?" he asks, quieter this time, but still agitated.

"I just had the giggles. We were fucking and then we were eating pizza in bed. It was funny. That's all. And then you went all crazy —"

"Crazy?" he screams, "Oh, now I'm fucking crazy," he shouts as he throws something at the wall. I bite my pillow to keep from screaming, and I keep my back to him. I pray that no one calls the MPs.

If the MPs come, I'll pretend it was the TV. Don't ever call him crazy.

He mutters and cusses and rolls over so his back is to mine. He mumbles things like "bitch" and "fucking crazy" and some other things I can't make out until, finally, he falls asleep. When I'm certain he's out, I tiptoe into the living room and fall asleep on the couch. The couch is less lonely.

In the morning, I wake up to him standing over me in his uniform. He's just come back from morning accountability formation.

"Why are you on the couch?"

"Do you not remember what happened last night?" He looks at me like I'm insane. He smirks at me like he always does when I'm being dramatic.

"Oh, that was nothing. I was just tired. I just wanted to know what you were laughing at."

You put your fucking hands on me.

I stare at him. He stares back, confused. I feel like I'm in *The Twilight Zone.*

"You good?" he asks.

No, I'm not good. And neither are you.

"Go get changed. I'll make us some chocolate chip pancakes."

I call my mother the next day. I know I can't tell her everything that's going on, but it'll be nice to hear a familiar voice.

"It must be good to have him home," she says.

"Yeah."

"Is he adjusting okay?"

"Yeah. I just — something's off."

"What do you mean?"

"He just seems off. Like his mind's somewhere else."

"Well, he did just get back from war, Alicia. You'd be a little off, too."

"Yeah, I suppose so."

"Why, has he done anything?"

"No," I lie.

"He's *adjusting*, Alicia. He's been through a lot and you just need to be there for him," she says, more stern this time, in the tone she uses when I'm being dramatic or making it all about me.

"I know. I'm just worried is all."

"The best thing you can do is be there for him."

5

THE DRAWING

When I was a kid, cable television was a luxury we enjoyed sporadically, and those periods of time often coincided with how much or little Dad was drinking. If he drank less, there was a cable box in the living room and in my bedroom, and Dad wouldn't whip out his pay stub when I asked for a candy bar at the register of the liquor store; he'd just say, "No," and leave it at that.

If he was drinking more, the cable box in the living room "went out," and Dad ended up watching the little box television in my bedroom. During those times, there was little more in our fridge than a bottle of mustard, some bologna, and a thirty-pack or two of Coors Light. If things were really tight, it was Busch or Keystone Light because they were cheaper. It was almost never the cans that just said "BEER," which were a true sign of desperation. It almost never got that bad.

On those nights, Dad sat at the foot of my sister's bed that was covered in a burgundy comforter, using a dining room chair or a stack of milk crates as a makeshift end table for his beer and ashtray. The plastic on our windows rustled with each draft of cold New England air that came through our windows. Dad had installed the plastic, poorly, as a way of keeping the house warm in the winter. He cut the plastic with a razor knife, which would have been fine, except that he had placed the plastic on cardboard on top of our bedspreads, so both of our comforters were slashed from where the razor knife had pierced through them.

Dad had the remote control, so instead of watching Nickelodeon or the Disney Channel like my sister, Amanda, and I usually did in *our* room, we mostly watched Bob Vila, nature or cooking shows, or *The Waltons*, which wasn't exactly ideal or stimulating programming for an eight- and a five-year-old. It wasn't until my mid-twenties — as I flipped back and forth between *Food Network*, *Animal Planet*, and *HGTV* — that I wished I could go back in time and smack my younger self for having such crap taste in television. As an adult, I realized that Dad's television line-up playing on one glorious loop was what I imagined heaven to be like.

In the evenings, Dad hunched over his end table, eating his dinner off the plate he'd crammed between his beers and ashtray. Amanda and I made sure we kept quiet, stayed out of the way, and brought Dad his beers, two at a time, each time he asked. He sat there, night after night, monopolizing our bedroom, and clinging to what was left of our cable service until, finally, the company cut it off completely.

One weekend afternoon, my parents sat me down to discuss a drawing I'd brought home from school earlier that week. I remember it being a weekend because we were home from school, and Dad had been home all day long, which meant he'd started drinking in the morning rather than waiting until the drive home from work in the late afternoon. The illustration seemed harmless enough: my teacher had asked us to draw a picture of us with our families at home, showing what a typical day looked like. My pencil-drawn stick figure family had faces filled in with bright yellow crayon. I drew a picture of myself holding up a paper with "100%" scrawled on the top, as I was stacking Legos with Amanda. Off to the side, Mom held a tray and wore a black apron, as she got ready to head to her job waiting tables, as she did most evenings. Dad sat on our brown couch with the orange and maroon floral pattern, watching TV, and holding a crudely drawn rectangle with the word "BEER" scribbled in red on it in one hand, and a cigarette with gray, squiggly line smoke in the other.

I drew them as my eight-year-old brain experienced them every day. Within two hours of being home from school, Mom always headed to work at a nearby Chinese restaurant, and she didn't come home until after I'd gone to sleep. All I knew about Dad was that he left in the mornings before I woke up for school, and at four o'clock, just before Mom needed to leave for work, he came home and sat on the couch, watched television, and drank beer, periodically yelled at Amanda and me to pipe down because, "This ain't *Romper Room*," until, finally, he either lost his temper about God-knows-what, or fell asleep, whichever came first.

"At least I come home every night," Dad said, usually to Mom if they were about to argue about his drinking. As a child, I felt proud of him because my dad loved me enough to come *home* after work and get wasted. He wasn't like other dads who went out for drinks after a long day on the job. They didn't love their kids as much as my dad loved me. Those dads belonged with those other parents who sent their kids to daycare or summer camp. I once asked my parents about both of them when I'd heard some kids at school talking about how much fun they had at *The Boys and Girls Club* after school or camp in the summertime.

"Why don't I go to daycare or summer camp?"

"Because we love you. *That's* why." Mom and Dad said that daycare and summer camp were for kids whose parents didn't want to spend time with them, so they sent them away with *strangers*, and I was just the luckiest little girl to have a mommy and a daddy who loved her enough to never send her away.

"Still want to go to summer camp?" Dad asked.

"No. I want to stay home with you."

"You sure? We can send you if you want. Maybe Mommy and Daddy can throw a party while you and your sister are out of the house."

"No!" I screamed, on the verge of tears, reassuring my parents that I loved them and I didn't want to be sent away with all the other cast-off little children. My parents threatened summer camp or daycare whenever we misbehaved, and that was usually enough to get us to straighten up.

They could have just told me that we didn't need daycare because one of them was always home to take care of us, and that they didn't have the money to send me to summer camp. I would have understood, and I'd have avoided a lot of trouble at school, since my teachers didn't appreciate me sharing with my classmates my newfound knowledge about the scores of unloved children being shipped off to daycares and summer camps.

Sure, Dad got hammered, and sometimes, he made a scene. Sometimes he and Mom fought, and maybe he took a swing at her. Maybe he started breaking things or trashing our house. Or maybe nothing happened. Maybe he just passed out. But Dad worked hard hauling sheetrock and hanging drywall so he could feed us, and clothe us, and keep a roof over our heads, and at the end of the day, he *chose* to come home to us and unwind. A drunk, unpredictable dad was better than no dad at all.

"Why is Daddy on the couch in your picture?" my parents asked me.

"Because that's all he does all day," and I proceeded to sit on the couch and kick my feet up with my hands behind my head. I don't remember the looks on their faces or what they said or did. I remember Amanda giggling. The conversation ended there, and I didn't think any more about it.

That evening, Mom made hamburgers and steak fries for dinner. Dad was watching figure skating all day, which I found really odd because I saw Dad as a brawny man's man, and a bunch of people ice-dancing in leotards didn't seem like his cup of tea. It was one of the oddly disarming things he did sometimes. His favorite movie was *The Sound of Music* and he had a crush on Julie Andrews, but not in the gross, perverse way that led to him talking about her "nice fart box," but in a boyish way that was adorable and endearing and left him blushing and left me hoping to someday be looked at the way Dad looked at Julie Andrews. He sang Disney tunes to himself all the time. He always knew when *Willy Wonka* or *The Wizard of Oz* were coming on and made a big deal about it. He once used breadcrumbs to help a duck and her ducklings get across Warwick Avenue safely. I can still see him: this tall, scary looking guy with a giant tattoo on his arm, tossing out breadcrumbs in the middle of the street, bringing traffic to a halt as a tiny group of ducks waddled across the street. I remember those moments where he'd display some random quirk, accidentally revealing his heart, and for a second, I wouldn't be afraid of him or intimidated by him. I'd just adore him and feel so lucky that he was mine.

Dad sat down with two beers and his dinner plate piled high with a mountain of steak fries, and two hamburger patties shoved between two slices of white sandwich bread, probably because we almost never had buns in the house. I remember sitting at our dinner table sometimes, with a boiled hot dog lying on a sad slice of white sandwich bread, asking why I couldn't have a hot dog bun instead.

"You got a bun right there," Mom or Dad said, pointing to my plate.

"No, this is *bread*."

"What do you think a bun's made out of? Fold it in half and eat your food."

Dad sat there in my room, staring at the TV, hunched over, devouring his dinner like someone was about to take it from him. I decided at that moment that I needed to get my diary out from under my mattress. I don't recall what was so urgent. I imagine it had something to do with a sudden realization about Dad's proximity to its hiding place, and I was consumed with a pang of paranoia that Dad would find it and I'd be in a heap of trouble.

I only ever wrote about two things in my diary: Boys I had crushes on, and musings on Dad's drinking and how I wish he would quit. Juicy stuff. I needed to move it in case he read the entries where I called him a "Butthead" or "Stupid face" for yelling at us so much, or the ones where I talked about Mark from my class and how I wanted to kiss him, maybe using tongues like they did in the movies. I wish I'd known then that Mom was the only one who read my diary, and that she would always find it no matter where I hid it. I'd have saved myself a lot of energy and aggravation. Once I had caught her reading it, my bed sheets in one hand and my innermost, private thoughts in her other.

"Mom, that's my diary!"

She snapped it shut and tossed it on the pile of bedding she was getting ready to wash.

"Oh, stop it. I'm just stripping the beds."

"Mom, I just saw you reading it."

"No, I wasn't. I'm doing laundry, Alicia. Nobody cares about your diary."

We always went back and forth like that. When I was little, I used to catch her smoking, which she hid from me because I'd learned in school that smoking was deadly, so naturally Mom couldn't smoke around me without me mourning the impending loss of my mother to lung cancer. I found her taking long, slow drags from her Marlboro Light. I would catch her red-handed, reeking of cigarette smoke or holding my open diary, but then she'd shout her vehement denials until she either exhausted me and I apologized to her, or she would convince me that I'd really just imagined the whole thing.

Anyway, with Dad preoccupied, Amanda helped me push the mattress up so I could retrieve my diary. I'd meant for us to lift it, but instead, our combined force slid the mattress off of the box spring, right in the direction of Dad's end table. The beer cans toppled over like dominoes, tipping a freshly opened beer over onto Dad's lap and wrecking his dinner. His eyes widened, fixing their glare in my direction. Just the way a dog bares its teeth right before an attack, Dad flared his nostrils.

"Son of a bitch." The boom of his voice made me jump. He raised his hand, smacking the contents of his end table all over my bedroom. He stood up, his left pant leg wet from where I'd injured him, and he was screaming and cursing, though I don't remember exactly what he was saying. I only recall feeling the jolt of his sudden, disproportionate reaction, and sitting on my bedroom floor with Amanda, our knees hugged into our chests because there was nowhere to run.

He loomed over us, red-faced and spitting while he shouted. He kept saying words like "ungrateful" and "disrespectful" and "spoiled brats," and I knew what they meant because those were the kinds of names Mom called us when we didn't clean up after ourselves or finish our dinner.

Mom stood in the doorway, her repeated pleas of "What happened?" being hushed by Dad's thunderous tirade. Finally, he stormed out of the room. Mom followed him, and we heard the crashing of plates and pans being thrown. Mom was flustered and confused.

"What happened? Raymond, what just happened?"

The echoes of shattering ceramic and glass continued.

"Ungrateful. Disrespectful. Spoiled brats."

It went on until Dad ran out of dishes to destroy, and I heard him stomp down the steps leading to our backyard.

Mom – shocked, confused, and out of breath – hurried into our room. My sister and I were still on the floor, whimpering and trembling. Amanda ran to Mom, and through my tears, I apologized to my mother for what I'd done.

"I'm sorry, Mommy. I moved the mattress by accident and I spilled the beer. I didn't mean to."

"It's okay. It was an accident. I'm going to go outside and talk to Dad. Everything's okay." She put Amanda down and went outside, and I found myself hoping that he wouldn't take whatever it was I did wrong out on Mom or her face.

I emerged from my bedroom to find the kitchen in ruins, its floor littered with shards of glass, our dinner, and fragments of what used to be our plates and bowls. I returned to my room and began picking fries, pieces of burger, and cigarette butts off of my bed and carpet. Now that Dad was outside, my dog, Misty, had come out of hiding, and was helping me by eating pieces of stray food off the floor. I grabbed a kitchen rag from under the sink so I could soak up the spilled beer from my comforter and rug.

After a while, Mom came back, looking slightly exasperated, but much calmer. She sat on my bed with me, and explained what happened.

"Daddy didn't mean to get so upset with you. I think your joke about your drawing today hurt his feelings."

"I didn't mean to spill the beer. It was an accident." I didn't understand.

"Daddy is outside crying right now. He said, 'My girls think I'm some lazy bum.' Do you think Daddy is lazy?"

"Only when he's at home." I still didn't understand.

"Doesn't Daddy work hard every day?"

"Yes."

"When he gets home, don't you think he's tired from working hard all day?"

"I guess so."

"So, is Daddy lazy?"

"No."

"Good girl. I think Daddy would really like a big hug and a kiss, and for both of you to tell him how much you love him."

I still didn't fully understand the chain of events of that evening, or how a spilled beer escalated into an impromptu kitchen demolition and reduced a grown man to tears. I only understood that I'd caused it, and I was wrong. I'd been taught right from wrong, and that when you're wrong, you apologize. When it came to me and my parents, it wasn't important to understand how, why, or even *if* I was wrong. I just needed to apologize.

We followed Mom outside to where Dad had been crying in the backyard. I walked toward him. He was sitting on the ground with his back against the side of our house and his knees hugged into his chest. There he was, the man who'd just cussed out his two small children because I'd accidently spilled his beer. Only it wasn't about the beer, but some other slight from earlier in the day that my eight-year-old brain still couldn't grasp. I needed to be still and calm because if he saw me trembling or crying, he'd get angry, which was less about the acts themselves and more about the way they made him hate himself, but I didn't know that yet.

As I approached him, I was afraid, but the only thing scarier than facing a grown man with a penchant for blind, irrational fits of rage was seeing him cry. I wrapped my tiny arms around his neck and kissed his tear-soaked, stubbly cheek, careful not to look him in the eye.

"I'm sorry, Daddy. I know you work really hard. I love you. Come back inside."

6

SHRAPNEL

On his way home from Afghanistan, my husband Chris smuggled some contraband. I discover this as I watch him unpack what I think is a belated anniversary gift. He pulls a flat, rectangular gift box out of his green duffle. He's wrapped it in aluminum foil and placed a blue bow in the center. The words, "Happy Anniversary, Hunny!" are scrawled in blue marker across the top. I grab the box and hold it up.

"For me?" I ask, excited that he's brought me something. He snatches the box from my hands.

"No. I just needed to get it home. Do you want to see it?"

I think he's brought home some souvenirs or something like that. I watch him slowly and carefully unwrap the foil. The box is filled with empty candy wrappers and potato chip bags to cushion what's inside.

"What is it?" I ask.

"Just wait." He grins as he hunches over the package, his eyes wide and alert, yet lifeless at the same time. He pulls out a piece of sharp, twisted metal. It's silver and dull and tarnished with black soot. He handles it carefully because some of the edges are jagged and sharp.

"What is it?"

"You remember that fire fight I was in?"

"Yes."

"This a piece of the RPG that hit us."

"Why would you save that?"

"Why *wouldn't* I?"

He grins harder. His eyes grow wider. I stop asking questions. I'm just a civilian; I wouldn't understand.

He places the shrapnel on a shelf in his closet where he keeps his Army coins and his socks. I see it every time I put away laundry. There it is. A twisted hunk of metal, no bigger than my fist, staring me in the face as it sits eye-level with me on the shelf. I have to be careful. He makes sure it's centered on the shelf. If it gets moved or disturbed when I put his socks away, he will know.

"Did you touch my shrapnel?"

"No."

"It's not where I left it."

"Yes, it is. I didn't touch anything."

"It wasn't centered. I always center it."

"I might have hit it while I was putting your socks away."

"Please don't mess with my things."

Okay, maybe you can get off your ass and put your own laundry away.

"Okay. Sorry."

Day in and day out, I straighten up the house, putting laundry away, the shrapnel reminding me that Chris is only here because of shitty aim and because the anti-personnel RPG hit a vehicle instead of my husband, the gunner sitting in the open turret. It taunts me with its presence: "Don't move me.

He'll know," the shrapnel says. "He won't let me out of his sight."

It never lets me forget how tightly they hold onto each other.

I watch Chris sit on the couch for what seems like days. I tell him to get out and get some fresh air, that it might do him some good. He tells me to stay in my fucking lane. I wonder how I've ended up with all of this laundry because I seldom see Chris bathe or change his clothes. He just sits on the couch, playing video games or staring into space. He cries out to me when he needs something or if the dog pisses on the floor. He screams at me for eating the last of the leftover salmon chowder. Then he locks me out of the bedroom and I sleep on the couch.

I lie on the opposite end from where he normally sits because he's made the cushions reek of body odor and sweat. But the smelly couch is still better than the bed. I can hear him cry out in his sleep, but I don't have to worry about him swatting or grabbing at me during a nightmare while the shrapnel hisses behind the closet door: "I am his. He is mine."

Well, he sure as shit isn't mine anymore.

I go to work each day and I come home to him exasperated on the couch, angrily fiddling away on his PlayStation controller and staring at the television as he speaks to me.

"The puppy. All day," he scolds.

"I'm sorry. She's still little, so it's a lot. I'll keep an eye on her."

"Lily needs to go out. Don't you see her by the door?"

"Okay, I just walked in. I'll let her out."

Lily pisses on the floor. "Are you fucking serious?" He screams.

"It's okay. I'll get it." I grab the paper towels and spray, and he starts moving toward the door.

"This has got to stop," he says, looming over me, watching me clean.

"Okay. It was an accident. What do you want me to do?"

"I want you to fucking contribute around here for once."

He returns to the couch, cussing and muttering about me under his breath. Just another standard, post-deployment afternoon.

I make his dinner and overcook it a little because a man can only call a woman a bitch or a cunt so many times before she decides to either poison him or burn his food. I can't change our current state or tell anyone what's going on, but I can ruin his dinner. He's different, and I'm different, and I often wonder which one of us I've come to hate more. He complains, but the reprimand is well worth the comforting little reminder that somewhere, deep beneath my new meek exterior, I'm still me.

I've taken to eating as little as possible because his new favorite thing is to take inventory of how much it costs to feed me. It's best to just eat a big lunch at work. I keep a bottle of wine hidden in the cabinet under the kitchen sink. I fill my tall, plastic, New England Patriots cup to the brim. I can't drink in front of him anymore. If I have so much as a beer or sip of wine in front of him, he berates me for being a "fucking drunk," to which I used to reply, "Not yet, but I'm getting there," just to piss him off. But I don't talk back anymore. He gets that look in his eye, the one where he's disappeared and whoever is left wants to chop my fucking head off. So, I hide my wine under the sink. Twenty ounces of Pinot Grigio is enough to fill the belly and thicken the skin.

I spend the nights doing chores. I walk past him as he toils away on his games. I carry a white plastic laundry basket under one arm and rest it on my hip. I clutch my cleverly disguised wine in my free hand the way a toddler clings to a security blanket. I hold my breath as I walk behind the couch to avoid his stench. I make my way into the bedroom with the dogs and lock myself in. I enjoy the peace and quiet while I fold laundry on the bed. I save his socks for last.

When he first got home, I loved doing the laundry. I was so happy to see his things in the wash again. I'd take his t-shirts out one by one and hug them to my chest while they were still warm. He was *home*. A few months later, I'm sitting on my bed with my laundry, locked in my bedroom with my dogs, staring at the pile of neatly folded t-shirts, wondering where the man that they belong to is. As I sip my wine, I see his pillow lying on the right side of the bed. I rest my head on it, inhaling deeply, trying to remember what he used to smell like, trying to remind myself that he's still here somewhere. I wonder how it's possible to sleep next to someone every night and still feel so fucking alone. I wonder if he feels alone, too. I wonder if I even care about how he feels anymore.

I hang up my work pants and blouses. I open Chris's closet and try to ignore the shrapnel as I place his shirts on the bottom shelf. I put his socks away to the right of the shrapnel and coins, careful not to disturb anything. I feel my face turn red and get warm.

"Hey. Hey!" He shouts from the living room."

"Yeah?"

"Answer me when I'm talking to you. Are the dogs with you?"

Who the fuck do you think you're talking to?

"Yeah."

"Thank you. Was that so hard?"

I grasp the front of the shelf, my forehead resting on the ledge. I see my dogs sit at my feet, a French bulldog and a baby pug look up at me with inquisitive head tilts.

I could leave. I could take them and leave. If he tries to fight it, I'll threaten to call the MPs. He won't make a scene if his job's on the line. Yeah, I'll just take the dogs and leave. Enough. He's gone.

I raise my head so my eyes meet the shrapnel. I gently press my index finger on one of its jagged points. He'll know, but I don't care. I curl my fingers around the whole thing. It fits in my hand. I hurl it at my mattress as hard as I can. It bounces. I pick it up and hurl it again. It feels important and monumental, what I'm doing. I pick up his pillow and press it against my face and scream as loudly as I can to drown out the shrapnel's heckling.

"I am his. He is mine."

I decide to pack a bag. I start piling my clothes in my black duffle. I'll pack it and I'll leave. Enough is enough. I pack enough for three days. Just to get me by until I figure out the rest.

You win, shrapnel. You win.

I place the shrapnel back on the shelf and close the door. I hide my bag under my side of the bed because I need to get some things out of the hallway closet.

Today is the day.

I walk toward the living room and see the back of his head facing the television. The racecar on the game he's playing has veered off the track and is driving into a wall.

What the hell kind of game is he playing anyway?

I walk closer to him. I see his hand by his side, lifeless on the couch cushion and the game controller next to him. His eyes are open, staring into space. I shake him.

"Honey, are you okay?"

He starts blinking and picks up his controller to resume his game.

"Yeah."

"What just happened?"

"What?"

"What just happened? You wandered off for a second."

"I guess I just spaced out. No big deal."

"I'm a little worried be —"

"Jesus, Alicia. I'm fine."

I go back to my bedroom and lock the door behind me. I go to my bed, and I snuggle my dogs as I lie on Chris's pillow. I scoop my cup of wine from the nightstand and finish it in one pronounced gulp. I open Chris's closet and see the shrapnel.

"I am his. He is mine."

I slide my duffle bag out from under the bed and unpack it. I hang up some of the clothes and I neatly fold the others and put them away.

"I am his. He is mine."

I press my finger on the sharp edge of the shrapnel. I press down hard, but it doesn't prick my finger. I shove it to the back of the closet and slam the door shut.

Actually, shrapnel, he's mine and I'm his. And you're just a fucking hunk of metal.

7

WARWICK AVENUE

S ummer in Warwick: it was stifling in the apartment because, even though we had an air conditioner, Mom and Dad never let us turn it on. We might get a few minutes here and there on the lowest setting, but not much. It was August, the hottest time of year, made worse because my parents didn't want to raise the electric bill. My sister, Amanda, and I sat in the living room in front of the fan, trying to cool off. She was nine and I was eleven. I could hear Mom and Dad's muffled arguing from the bathroom.

"This is who I am," Dad said.

"That's not who you are. That's your mother talking," Mom fired back.

I turned the volume knob on the television higher so Amanda wouldn't be able to hear them. I walked toward the entrance of the hallway so I could hear them better while still keeping an eye on Amanda as she clutched her crocheted bunny and watched cartoons.

"I won't change who I am," Dad said.

"That's not who you are, Raymond," Mom replied, "But if

you're going to be drinking, then you need to leave for these girls."

"I love my kids," Dad shouted.

Amanda jumped, and I turned up the volume on the television even louder.

"If you love these girls, then you'll leave."

Three days earlier, my mother had sobbed on our black and yellow sofa that we referred to as the bumble bee couch, not only because of its pattern, but because of the pointy metal rod that poked out from a hole in the middle seat that left a nasty welt on your back if you sat down without paying attention. I still think about that couch when Mom complains that my sister needs new furniture and needs to paint her living room.

Okay, Mom.

I watched Mom reason back and forth that day, clutching the cordless phone to her ear, saying things like, "I love you, too," and "You've got to stop for these girls." Dad had drunk-dialed from Grandma's again, no doubt crying about how much he missed us and promising that if Mom let him move back home, he'd change. He'd quit drinking on his own. He'd say he didn't need rehab. Mom would remind him that he'd tried to stop before, but it had always ended the same way. I listened to her repeat the same conversation I'd heard so many times over the years. I listened to her use the same words and present the same argument that would devolve into her using my sister and me as a bargaining chip. That usually worked. Dad would choose drinking over a lot of things, but not us. "It's the drinking or your kids," was usually a solid ultimatum that could buy us at least a few sober weeks.

Mom finally hung up the phone and held her head in her hands. I stood there and waited for her to get it together, hoping that she wouldn't ask me for comfort or for a hug. She always left a snot trail on my neck and shoulder when she cried.

Anyway, comfort and reassurance was supposed to be *her* job, but there I was, having to hug her every time Dad smacked her across the face or threw his keys or the remote control at her. I'd tell her that I was scared of Dad, and she'd tell me that I was being ridiculous, that my father would *never* lay a hand on me. I wondered how someone who couldn't protect herself had any business reassuring me of my safety.

"Come give your mother a hug," she whimpered.

Here we go.

I sat next to her and held her while she wailed in my ear at a volume that I thought was a little loud for the situation, but maybe I was being cold. After all, I was the same kid who a few months before had watched Dad break my recorder over Mom's head and, instead of rushing to my mother's aid, had become indignant.

"My recorder! You broke it!" I screamed as I collected the shattered remnants of my little woodwind instrument off the dining room floor.

"Oh, stop it. I'll buy you another fucking recorder," Dad sneered.

"No, you won't," I mumbled as I stomped off to my room. Mom's well-being was the furthest thing from my mind. Things like that had become pretty normal; I guess that was part of the problem.

By that time, Dad had been gone for two months. Things weren't easy. Dad had taken Grandma's advice to cut us off financially: "Don't pay her a dime," she had told him. "She'll take you back real quick." Things were tight, but we were okay. Anyway, life without Dad in the house was easier.

"I don't know what to do, Alicia," Mom cried.

And I do? I'm eleven.

"He sounded so sad. He misses you girls," she continued.

He always does.

"He said he'll quit drinking if he can come home."

He usually does.

"What do you think, Lee?"

I'm eleven.

"What should I do, Lee?" She looked at me as if I were an adult. Even then, I knew that this was not my area, that I was ill-equipped to answer this question. I remember my face getting hot as I clenched my fists because it felt unfair of her to put this on me. I remember hating her because even I knew that things would end the same, and I couldn't understand how she could be so stupid. I was angry because I was eleven, and it felt like I knew everything and that I knew nothing, and I wanted just one adult to have the answers so I wouldn't have to answer stupid questions like whether or not my mother should let my alcoholic father come home.

"I think he should stay at Grandma's," I said.

"You do?"

"He won't stop drinking. He'll stop for a few days and go back like he always does."

"Are you happier with Dad at Grandma's?"

I paused for a moment. I knew that whatever I said, it would make its way back to Dad. Nothing was sacred when it came to Mom. It'd be like when I told her I got my period and not to tell Dad, and a week later, we'd be at Friendly's eating ice cream, while Mom proudly declared, "Alicia has become a woman," and Dad held his head in his hands, and I sat there, flushed and fucking mortified, feeling the need to apologize for my menstruation.

If I said no, he'd come home and Mom would use me to validate the very stupid decision to let him come home. If I said yes, Dad might not come home, but he'd know that I said I liked life better without him. And I'd never hear the end of it. And

Mom would say that she got rid of him for me. But he'd be gone, and maybe we'd have a chance.

"Yes," I said. I knew there'd be consequences, but I had to try. Someone had to be an adult.

"You are?"

"Yes. I think Amanda is, too. I think things are better without him."

"Really?"

"If he comes home, it'll go back to the way it was before. Don't let him come home." I was calm when I said the words, knowing that I'd have to own them regardless. Mom didn't expect me to say them. Dad would see them as a betrayal. They probably didn't belong together anyway, but it would fall on me.

Mom looked at me and broke into hysterics again. She held her head in her hands and sobbed and turned on the theatrics, like what I had said was somehow new information. I was eleven. He was a drunk. He was loud and mean and careless, and I'd seen him hit my mother on more than one occasion. And what was worse was that Amanda and I were starting to think it was normal.

She looked at me again without saying anything. She picked up the phone and began to dial, and I held my breath as I waited for her to tell Dad what I'd said. He'd be mad at me, but it would be worth it.

"Come home before I change my mind," she said into the receiver and hung up.

Mom stared at me, scanning my face for a reaction. I clenched my fists once more and calmly walked away, bracing myself for Dad's return home. I sat on my bed waiting as I heard Mom and Amanda rejoicing in the living room.

"Daddy's coming home!"

I could hear Amanda squealing with excitement, but I

wasn't angry at her. She didn't know any better. Mom knew better.

Twenty minutes later, Dad stumbled through the door, wasted as usual. He held a six-pack of O'Doul's in his hand. "These don't have any alcohol in them. I'm switching to these tomorrow," he slurred. I sat at our computer desk, pretending to play Solitaire. Amanda sat on Dad's lap as he smiled at the room, glassy-eyed and puffing a Newport in his free hand.

"Oh, you've got to see this thing Alicia does, Raymond. It's hysterical," Mom said.

"I don't feel like doing it right now," I grumbled.

"Oh, come on. You have to show him."

"Not right now," I muttered, never turning my gaze away from the computer screen. Mom ignored me and inserted the Celine Dion CD in the stereo and put on, "When I Need You."

"Come on, Alicia. Do it."

She was asking me to do this theatrical lip sync that I did for her and my aunts that they all thought was really funny. Dad would just be pissed about all the noise. Historically, my father didn't find much of anything I did very funny, and the last thing I wanted to do was put on a show for my wasted father who, I'd just told my mother, I didn't want in my house. The last thing Dad needed was a reminder of how outspoken and hilarious I got when he left for a while; it made him hate himself, but Mom already knew that. It would be just as painful for him as it would be for me.

The track started to play, and like a trained monkey, I got up and performed for my father as my mother laughed and Dad sat there stone-faced, just like I knew he would.

"Isn't she hysterical?" Mom asked.

"Mmhmm," Dad muttered, his gaze still stern and serious.

I hate you both so much.

Dad made it three days with the O'Doul's. I knew he

wouldn't make it for very long, but the unfortunate thing about Dad's sobriety was how quickly it grew on me anyway. I liked not having to check his breathing after he passed out on the couch. I liked the way he hugged me when he got home from work, not pushing me away prematurely so he could grab a beer out of the fridge. I liked the way he and Mom got along and how he didn't fly off the handle unprovoked. I liked the peace and quiet. I liked the way a day came and went, and didn't devolve into Dad chain-smoking on the couch, mumbling, and feeling sorry for himself. I knew it wouldn't last, but once I had it, I found myself praying every night that I was wrong.

Please, prove me wrong. Please let this last forever.

Amanda and I sat on the living room floor as Dad carried laundry baskets of his things outside to his truck. I stood by the sliding glass doors and watched Dad go back and forth between the apartment and his truck. Amanda started clutching her bunny and crying. She scurried into the bathroom to be with Mom. I watched Dad continue to pack his things while he never once looked up at me. When he was finished, he sat down in the living room with me and my sister, who was still crying.

"Daddy's going back to Grandma's house. It's just not working out."

I knew it wouldn't.

"Mommy and Daddy just grew apart," he continued.

No. You're a drunk.

"But that has nothing to do with how much we love you girls."

Nah. You're just choosing beer over us. I'll try not to take it personally.

I remember Dad hugged us both. He brought one last load of his stuff out to his truck, and as I watched from the glass door, Mom walked up behind me and stood over my shoulder.

"I'm so sorry, Alicia."

"I hate you."

I said it calmly, without clenched teeth or a hint of disdain or adolescent outburst. I said it matter-of-factly, like it was just another thing about me, like my brown eyes or my long hair. Mom walked away.

What happened next is still hazy in my memory. Mom still had to go to work, and Dad loaded us in his truck, stopped at the drive-through liquor store for a thirty-pack, and we all spent the night at Grandma's house. Mom and Amanda agree that this is how it happened. The timeline makes sense, but that's not what I remember.

Instead, I remember standing by the sliding glass doors, watching Dad pack the remainder of his life with us into his red Mitsubishi pickup truck. I waited for him to look back, but he didn't. Instead, he started his truck, and I heard the loud roar of the engine and that clunking noise the truck always made because the muffler was missing. He pulled away, and still, I waited for him to look back. I was alone in the living room, watching Dad drive off. I followed the shadow of his truck through the hedges that blocked the side road in front of our apartment. When he was out of sight, I listened for the sound of his beat-up truck, as it slowed to a stop at the intersection that led to the main road. I waited for the roar to grow louder again, because I'd half expected him to turn around and come back. He'd chosen drinking over a lot of things, but he wouldn't choose it over us. The truck hummed steadily at the red light. I heard the engine roar once more as the light turned green, and I listened as the truck's sound disappeared among the rush hour traffic of Warwick Avenue.

8

DEPENDA

His haircut gives him away. People can tell just by his medium fade that he was a soldier. Since we'd gotten back to Georgia, he gets jumpy as people approach asking, "Excuse me, are you in the service?" We came back to Georgia nine months after his return from Afghanistan. We were supposed to move back the following February, but Chris was growing more and more tired of his job and the people he worked with. He'd done a good job of keeping his crazy under wraps, only acting out around me and being his most functional at work. As time went on, I could see cracks forming when it came to work and his impatience with his platoon. He'd mouthed off to a First Sergeant, demanding he answer for not helping the soldiers under him, and by pure luck and mercy, this impressed the First Sergeant enough for him to promote Chris to Corporal Barksdale.

He told me this story one September afternoon, sounding pleased with himself, like he was untouchable. I knew better. All he needed to do was piss off the wrong person, and work would be just as bad as home.

"I'm so fucking sick of this place," he said.

"I think it's time for us to go home. Can you put in for us to leave early?"

He put in the paperwork, and we left Germany right before Christmas. I thought going back to Savannah would do him some good. I thought being around his family would help him through whatever he was going through. I thought the warmer temperatures and sunshine of the lowcountry would bring him back to life, and maybe we could get back to being the people we used to be. But you know what they say: Wherever you go, there you are.

In Germany, they spent a lot of time talking about OPSEC [Operational Security] and how we should do everything we could to blend in: No "ARMY WIFE" bumper stickers on our cars, no wearing anything that let people know we were affiliated with the military, no going anywhere in uniform. "Loose lips sink ships," was the motto. They used to run this television PSA about OPSEC on the Armed Forces Network that involved some person decked out in camouflage and wielding a sniper rifle who lurked just off post, waiting to take down anyone affiliated with the military.

"Oh, my god! We have to worry about snipers?" I cried. I was a new military wife then and Chris hadn't deployed yet. And I didn't have to worry so much about snipers as I did other wives. One day, I went to replace my car battery at the store that just so happened to be near the barracks, and by the next time I talked to my husband over video chat, the news of his wife hanging around the barracks had already made its way to him in Afghanistan.

"Alicia, there aren't any snipers trying to get you," Chris had said.

"It was on the commercial on AFN. I'm gonna get snipered if I go off post."

"Sweetie, they just want you to be careful. That's not going to happen, and snipered isn't a word," he laughed.

But that was before. And now we're in the after, and my husband flinches as an older man stops him in a Kohl's to shake his hand and thank him for his service. I watch him nod cautiously, thanking the man for acknowledging him. The man turns to me. "And you too, Ma'am. Thank you."

"Oh, I'm not in the military."

"But Ma'am, you stood by this young man. Thank you for all you've done." I stop arguing and shake his hand.

This happens all the time. I usually wander away when someone approaches Chris to thank him. If not, they'll turn to thank me, and I'll have to do the dance where I tell them I've done nothing, which is a reflex. I'll politely concede, because that's what I'm supposed to do. I'll refrain from shaking their hands firmly, and giving an emphatic, "You're welcome," for fear of being labeled a dependa, which is a term someone made up to describe lazy, entitled military wives who wear their husbands' ranks and accomplishments. But somehow it started getting used to describe all of us lowly spouses, or "dependents," as the Army calls us. So, I smile, and I look down, and I shake peoples' hands, and when Chris and I leave, I'll say, "That was nice. I don't know why they shake *my* hand, though. You did all the work," hoping that it'll make him smile and feel good about himself, and half hoping that he'll say, "I know why."

We're back in America now, and Georgia supports their troops. Any day of the week, Chris can get a free meal, or a discount, or a military deal on a new set of wheels. Store clerks ask me if I'm military and I reply, "No. My husband is." The man asks him where he deployed to and where he was stationed. Chris talks about COP Zormat and the MP night missions and the detainees, and they swap war stories. I stand close by as some old man tells my husband what a great young man he is. I sift through clothing racks while I think to myself, "He sure used to be."

"Wow, a gunner. What was that like?" the man asks, and I remember Chris starting to tell me about it before our first trip to Behavioral Health. How he just kept firing from the open turret. How he reached out for some ammo and for a split second, he was afraid that he might lose his hand.

"Okay, talk to the counselor about that. Tell her about the nightmares and the irritability and the spacing out. Nothing about you and me, got it?" I told him.

"Nothing?" He was confused because I told him to get help or move out.

"You can tell her that it's putting a strain on our marriage. Keep it at that. But nothing about the blackouts or the hair pulling thing, okay?"

"Are you sure?"

"They'll go to your chain of command. Now, repeat it back to me."

But he's talking about his wrist surgery now. Talking about the titanium plate he has in there and the three or four surgeries it took to get there. And funniest thing, he broke it the week before deployment during a game of touch football, and wouldn't you know it, the guy who broke it is now our brother-in-law.

"You deployed with a broken wrist? As a *gunner*?"

The man is so impressed with how he fought the terrorists one-handed. It's enough to make you want to stand up with your fist in the air and shout "'Merica!" while an eagle soars overhead. I'll laugh to myself when they tell him how badass he is.

His chain of command wouldn't let him get that wrist treated, and then they lied about it. He had to wait a year and a half. Then they fucked it up. Now he's got bone degeneration, ligament damage, arthritis, carpal tunnel, and he thinks everyone's out to get him. Badass, huh brother?

He leaves out the day in Landstuhl when he tried to eat a turkey wrap one-handed after surgery. He won't tell him how he got frustrated like a grouchy toddler and smacked the wrap all over the table and how I cleaned it up while he bitched about "this fucking cast." He mentions the four-hour drives to and from Landstuhl for his follow-up visits, and that I drove him, but he leaves out the part where he screamed at me while I tried to drive on the autobahn, calling me a "dumb bitch" and a "stupid cunt" for hours, until he made me pull over, and took the keys from me, and drove the rest of the way going 100 miles per hour with one arm and a belly full of Norco. I make sure we both keep that part to ourselves.

"What made you get out?" he asks, wanting to know why Chris gave up the military life. He tells him how he wanted to stay in the same place and get a good steady government job. He leaves out the part where I told him I wouldn't have kids with him if he reenlisted. He won't tell him about how I pleaded with him every time the subject came up. "You've given enough," I said, and that usually ended the discussion. Sometimes he kept going, trying to convince me just how "fine" he was, and I reminded him that men who were fine didn't keel over and hyperventilate on their back patios when they hear the crackle of 4th of July fireworks in the distance. Men who were fine didn't need their wives to stand behind them, reminding them to breathe, and softly repeating, "It's only fireworks. They're only fireworks," over and over again until they believed it.

"You couldn't handle one deployment. What makes you think you can keep going for another fifteen years?" I asked.

He gave me that sad look, like he'd just learned my deep

dark secret. I regretted the words as soon as they came out, not because I didn't mean them, but because not every truth needed to be said out loud.

"They give you a disability rating?" the man asks, and I shake my head as Chris answers "90 percent," because on what planet is that an appropriate thing to ask someone? Nobody goes up to someone and asks, "How much do you make?" In the end, a panel of strangers sat down with my husband's medical history and determined that a bum wrist, traumatic brain injury, PTSD, night terrors, folliculitis, erectile dysfunction from 40mg of Prozac per day, and chronic, sometimes crippling anxiety were worth $2,100 a month for life. If he adds in the sleep apnea he was recently diagnosed with, and he redoes his paperwork, he could get a full disability rating and be sitting pretty at $3,200 per month. Which would take him from $25,200 per year to $38,400, the going rate for a man's soul, free money from the government that we should be grateful for. A few grand a year to honor his sacrifice to our country. And when I think of what he gave in exchange, I can't help but think he's been lowballed.

I remember him being a year or so from getting out, triggered by something that led to a three-week manic episode. "Get help or get out," I finally said, because in the after, ultimatums were the only way to get things done.

"Don't tell them about the fit in the car or trying to leave me in the parking lot," I reminded him. I had lied to the social worker on the phone. "No, he's just having a tough time," because it occurred to me that they were trying to diagnose him as bipolar, and if they did, they might have said he enlisted that way. He wasn't bipolar, but they would try to say he was anyway. They could've discharged him for it. They could've taken away his benefits and his retirement. Everything he'd worked for during the last six years. And then all of this would have been for nothing. $2,100 a month wasn't much. Hell, it was insulting. But it was something. And something was better than nothing.

"This is not what your husband has been telling us," the social worker said.

"He's been anxious lately. He's got a lot going on. Work's been crazy," I lied.

"What he's describing sounds like a manic episode."

"No. He just likes to keep his hands busy when he's anxious. At least he's gotten a lot done in the yard," I joked.

I listened as they talked about doubling his Prozac. They were going to numb him even more. I decided that we could deal with this once he was out and the VA had given him his due.

Something was better than nothing.

He came home that day, frustrated and confused. He found me in the living room, folding laundry. Wide eyed, he asked, "What the hell was that? What *happened*? You're the one who told me to go get help."

I didn't look up at him.

"When you get out, we'll get you some *real* help from a *real* counselor, okay?"

He looked at me. I continued folding laundry.

"Trust me, I just did you a favor. You're welcome."

Now the man shakes our hands again, and we head home. I start putting away all the items from the day's haul. I tidy up while Chris takes the dogs out. I pull out my new Lion King t-shirts that Chris lets me compulsively buy and hug each one to my chest because they help me remember only the very best moments with my father. I start folding clothes and putting away stray items around our bedroom. I see Chris's watch, the one I gave him the day he returned from Afghanistan, and I pick it up to put it in a safe place. I open the top drawer of his nightstand and see a clear, square Tupperware container. I hold my breath as I remove the clear blue lid, preparing to find moldy remnants of an old snack.

I swear, if he's hoarding dirty dishes in his nightstand, I'll —

And just before I finish cursing my husband for eating in the bedroom, I see a tiny opened envelope, that says SUGAR PEEN. It's a small card I'd placed in his lunch bag a few months before. Beneath that is an ugly, broken seashell from a trip to the beach we'd taken together years before. I remember him picking it up. "That's an ugly shell," I said.

"I like it," he said, putting the seashell fragment in his pocket.

Beneath that is a clear bag containing a red washcloth that is soaked in my perfume. I sent it to him five years before, right when he first arrived in Afghanistan. Someone told me to send him something that smelled like me.

"This is dumb," I had said when I sprayed a red washcloth with Clinique Happy perfume.

"Just what he needs; a bunch of smelly crap he can't use."

I didn't know he had kept it. I'd always assumed he'd thrown it away.

Beneath that is the first letter I'd sent him while he was deployed, telling him how proud I was and how I couldn't wait for him to get home. There are also stacks of pictures, mostly of me, and some from our wedding day. He has an orange lighter that he'd used downrange. There are three black diamonds that he'd gotten for me, and promised to have set in a piece of jewelry, but never did. And finally, a small sticky note that my sister sent to him while he was in basic training, after I'd told her how he called me crying and begging for me to get him out of there. It was a bible verse from Hebrews 12:1 that read

Let us run

> *with*
>
> *perseverance*
>
> *the race*
>
> *that is set before us.*

I sit on my bed, the items strewn over Chris's side of the comforter.

"Sweetie, where you at?" I hear him shout from the kitchen. He's in the doorway and I look up at him with tears in my eyes.

"You found my treasures," he smiles.

"I'm sorry. I was putting your watch away and I thought it was old food."

"No. That's my treasure box," he says as he sits beside me, carefully putting each item back into its place.

"Have you always had that?" I ask.

"Since Germany. So, for a while," he shrugs.

"And you just keep it here?"

"Yeah. Unless I travel. Then I take it with me."

A tear runs down my cheek.

"Oh, no. What?" he asks, looking the way he does when he thinks he's in trouble.

I kiss his forehead.

"Thank you."

"You're welcome?" he says, still confused.

Maybe he does know why they thank me. That's something, at least.

Something is better than nothing.

9

THE DRESSER

As I entered Dad's bedroom to help him pick out an outfit for dinner, I choked on the air, thick with the musty stench of dirty laundry, beer, and cheap menthol cigarettes. Through the heaps of soiled undergarments and crushed beer cans, a decent-looking hardwood floor was peeking out. A thin layer of ash and cookie crumbs blanketed every inch of the tiny space, and Dad rushed over to his unmade bed — a thin mattress and box spring resting on the floor — to sweep a pile of crumbs onto the floor.

"Sorry, I didn't get a chance to tidy up," Dad said with a smile. To the right of his bed stood a TV tray serving as a makeshift nightstand. On top was a yellow glass ashtray, overflowing with cigarette butts. The crushed pile of Mavericks cigarette boxes was spilling onto the floor.

Dad rifled through one of the piles of clothing. "Alright, I gotta have something in here," he said. I scanned the room for the cleanest looking pile of clothes and I reluctantly joined the search for a presentable dinner outfit. As I rummaged through the clothes, the ripe smell of feet hit me right away.

My sister, Amanda, was at the opposite corner of the room. "I found pants," she declared. Searching through that shithole had turned into a smelly scavenger hunt.

"Nah, those are ripped, Kid," Dad said. He continued to hold his beer in one hand and sift through the clothing with the other.

"Okay, here we go," he said, holding up a pair of oversized polo shirts, one an awful shade of teal and the other the color of pea soup.

"Which one?" he asked me. The shirts belonged to my grandmother's dead husband, who was easily three shirt sizes larger than my father. I could hear Uncle Stephen in the living room, telling Dad that he might have a shirt for him. I'd spent the first half of our visit listening to Uncle Stephen tell a story with a knife in one hand and a pipe in the other, bragging about how he'd chased someone down the street with them a few nights before. He was pudgy and shirtless, and the remnants of his lunch were mangled in his curly chest hairs.

"Ray, I got a shirt for ya. Let me go get it. It's beautiful," he said. I knew it was going to be an awful bowling shirt, but at least it would fit him. Dad removed his shirt, revealing a swollen beer belly and a purple bite mark on his chest.

"Did you do that to him?" Amanda said, looking at Uncle Stephen with disgust as he laughed and my father stared at the ground.

"I see you two are getting along," Amanda said, pointing to Dad's black eye.

"Oh, we always get along," Dad mumbled, still staring at the ground.

After Dad settled on an outfit, my sister started searching for clean socks. I walked around the room, immune to the stench, and examined the space that Dad called home.

"Someone must've stolen his bike again," Amanda said as

she pointed to the empty corner of Dad's room. Dad lost his driver's license years before from one too many DUI's and used a bike to get to and from the liquor store. He'd mastered riding his bike with one hand while balancing a 30-pack in the other.

I examined the room, disgusted that a human being lived like this. I'm not sure if it was the state of the room that upset me or if it was the fact that my father occupied it. *This* was what he left us for?

"This is actually pretty clean for him," Amanda said, bringing me back to the filthy bedroom.

"Seriously?"

"Cookie must've been here recently," she said, pointing to a newer looking pair of sneakers on the floor. Cookie was my father's off-and-on companion. They had married ten years before, but the marriage wasn't legal because she was already married to someone else. I'd only met her once when I was a kid. She was tall and pale with bleach-blonde hair, her face caved in where her teeth used to be. She had a home confinement bracelet on her right ankle, undoubtedly related to any one of her dozens of criminal offenses we read about on the Rhode Island Judiciary website. When Amanda and I stopped going to visit Dad on the weekends, he married her.

"Cookie comes around every now and again, and Dad will sleep with her and she'll give him money or new sneakers," Amanda said.

"Are you kidding me?"

"No. She's with some old guy now. But Dad calls her when he's lonely. Lee, see if there are any socks in the dresser," Amanda ordered.

On the left side of the room stood a dark mahogany dresser with a large mirror in the center. As I leaned down to grab the knob of the top drawer, I was halted by the sight on top of the dresser. The top was clean and polished, lacking the dust and ash that resided throughout the rest of the room. Placed neatly in the center were pictures of my sister and me. On the left was a 5 x 7 of my kindergarten class photo. In the center, a photo collage of my sister and me, plastered with pictures spanning from grade school through high school. Pictures of us reminded him of the years he'd missed, and that we'd grown up without him. There was a newspaper clipping from when Amanda made the sixth-grade honor roll. To the right stood a "World's Greatest Dad" certificate that we had given Dad when we were little. The photos were free of dust and smudges and stood neatly. The certificate was over twenty years old, without so much as a fold or crease. The display had been cared for and dusted regularly, and while the rest of the room was covered in ruins of filthy clothes, ash, and trash, our pictures sat gleaming and pristine, his only prized possessions.

We took Dad to Bassett's Inn for dinner. Well, it used to be called that. It was under new ownership with a new name by then, though I don't recall what that was. I watched him shakily spoon chowder into his mouth, and longed for the time when he could eat mounds of food that never seemed to fatten him up. I missed him trying to snatch from my plate. He took me to that restaurant for dinner when I was thirteen and we had spent the night making fun of the hostess, who bore a striking resemblance to Annie Lennox. When I rattled off, "*Sweet dreams are made of this,*" I was certain Dad would scold me for misbehaving. He looked at me, first wondering how I knew that song, then looked at the hostess and burst into laughter.

"*Travel the world and the seven seas,*" he sang back as we struggled to contain ourselves. We usually ate in silence at restaurants. Dad was big on kids being seen and not heard in public, and he and Mom prided themselves on our obedience. Any other night, he would have yelled at me and threatened to never take me out again, but that was a good night. I didn't recall many nights where my father and I laughed about anything.

After dinner, we took Dad to see *The Lion King*. We had seen it with him as kids, and it was our favorite movie to watch together. It just so happened that the movie was playing during my visit, at the same theater we'd seen it in as kids. I couldn't resist the urge to take him to see it with Amanda and me — just the three of us. I hadn't seen him in nearly six years, and I remember thinking how the timing was perfect. What a great way to spend our time together.

As the night was winding down, we drove past our old house on Warwick Avenue. "A lot of good memories," Dad said. Then later, as we chatted over drinks at a local bar, Dad got serious.

"I know you have a lot of bad memories, but you have a lot of good ones, too," he said. It was clear to me that Dad's version of history was different from mine. When he saw the house on Warwick Ave, he was seeing the place where he had taught me to ride a bike and play ball. He saw that spot in the yard where our lopsided pool stood for two summers. He saw the Christmas tree that he screwed up by sawing from the top instead of the bottom, remembering our laughter over the trapezoid shape that we decorated. He didn't remember locking Mom out of the house that time she forgot to wash his socks. He didn't see the dining room he trashed one night after he thought Mom was checking out some guy. I was sure he remembered all of it like I did, but unlike me, that wasn't all he remembered. It occurred to me that Dad's recollections were more complete than mine. Dad sat across the table from me, his eyes urging me to remember the good times, and my heart broke.

"I know, Dad. Remember that one father/daughter dance that we had at home?" His eyes widened and he seemed relieved as I talked about the school father/daughter dance we had to miss in fifth grade because Amanda was sent home sick from school. Dad went to the store and bought lobster and steaks, which was definitely above our means, and he had cooked us an amazing meal. He put on his suit and danced with us over candlelight in the dining room. We spent the evening listening to our Disney songs, laughing and dancing as he told us how a date night with his girls was better than any old, boring dance at the school.

"That was a good night, Kid. Your old man ain't so bad, huh?"

"It was a good night, Dad. You did good," I said as I held his hand across the table.

A year and a half later, Dad died. I flew back to Rhode Island and entered the house that had so disgusted me before. Uncle Stephen was in prison and my grandmother was sitting in her chair, looking as frail as possible, and talking about "her Raymond" and asking, "What about me? What do I do now?" I asked my Uncle Kevin to meet me at the house to help me get Dad's ID for the funeral home. The neighborhood crack-head sat next to my grandmother.

"He was my best friend," he cried.

"I know, Cappy."

"He just *loved* you girls so much."

I returned to Dad's bedroom. The mattress had slid halfway off the box spring when the paramedics had dragged Dad off the bed and tried to revive him. The heaps of clothes and trash were there, but the mounds seemed larger and the space infinitely smaller. The stench of stale cigarettes, beer, and dirty feet lingered in the air, but failed to choke me. Dad's pillow held the indent from his giant head. I ran my fingers gently along the outline in the pillow, careful not to disturb the imprint. In the previously empty corner, I saw the new bike that Dad had told me about on the phone a few days earlier. I tiptoed through empty beer cans, dirty underwear, and crumpled papers toward the bike. Dad's jackets neatly hung from the right handlebar. I unhooked his old leather jacket from the handle and buried my face in it, inhaling deeply. As I closed my eyes and took in the scent of cologne and Newports, I heard Uncle Kevin shouting from the living room, "This is fucking disgusting. Who fucking lives like this?" and I was comforted by the thought that someone else knew that Dad had deserved better.

I gathered Dad's jackets, a hammer, and a hoodie that smelled like him. There was nothing else in the room for me to take besides dirty underwear and beer cans. I moved to the left side of the room to find that the dresser had disappeared. I stormed into the living room where Uncle Kevin had secured Dad's expired driver's license and Carpenter's Union ID in a plastic Jeff Gordon helmet that Dad kept beside his bed.

"Where's the dresser?"

"What dresser?" Grandma asked.

"The dresser. The one that used to be in his room. Where is it?"

"Oh, I don't know."

"How do you lose a fucking dresser? Where is it?"

"Oh, Stephen probably took it. He ransacked the house while I was in the hospital and took everything." Uncle Stephen had a habit of robbing the house for drug money. That was business as usual.

"Where are Dad's pictures?"

"What pictures?"

"He had pictures of Amanda and me. Where are they?"

"I don't know about any pictures," she said.

Uncle Kevin helped me gather Dad's things and assured me that's all he could find. I let Grandma know I'd be back in a few days to pick up Dad's suit and to let Amanda visit. As I loaded the car, an older gentleman, a neighbor, approached me.

"Are you Ray's daughter?"

"Yes, I am. I'm Alicia."

"You look like your sister."

"Amanda. People say we look alike."

"I'm very sorry about Ray. It's a damn shame. He was a good guy."

"Thank you. He sure was."

"He talked about you girls all the time. You made him real proud."

* * *

Amanda arrived a few days later and we returned to the house. Amanda, more familiar with the surroundings, led me to the basement.

"Wow, Uncle took everything. All of Dad's tools are gone."

There was a pile of broken glass, sheets, and garbage bags in the middle of the floor. On the wall was a framed, felt picture of Jeff Gordon's Dupont race car. Amanda or I had given it to Dad as a present, but neither of us recalled the who or when of the gift. Amanda ripped the picture off the wall and took it upstairs.

We sat down on the couch while Grandma and the crackhead started talking about Dad, and Grandma started complaining that my grandfather was having a gathering for Dad without inviting her. We tuned her out. Amanda opened the coffee table drawer and sifted through a half dozen cell phones. Dad used to hoard cell phones. He'd brag about how he got free minutes from promotions, but when the promotion was over, he'd get a new phone with free minutes. She pulled a card out.

"Here's Dad's food stamp card. Someone will need to call and cancel it," she said.

"I can get another $200 out of that," Grandma said.

"I'll take care of it," Amanda said, putting the card in her pocket. She then pulled a lighter and Dad's phone book from the drawer.

"I'd like to keep this book," Amanda said as she handed me the lighter. She flipped the book to the first page. In Dad's chicken scratch were Mom's, Amanda's and my phone numbers.

I waited in the living room, nodding and smiling at Grandma's ramblings while Amanda walked through Dad's bedroom one last time. She wasn't looking for anything in particular. I knew that coming back to the house meant something more to her. I didn't know then what peace she was trying to find there. I just knew it didn't involve me, and I let her wander through the house by herself.

"You were asking about pictures the other day. Are those them?" Grandma asked as she pointed above the TV stand. Mounted to the wall were the same photos from the dresser. The collage, my kindergarten photo. "That's them!" I snatched the frames from the wall and tucked them under my arm.

When Amanda was through, we left. As we drove through the streets of Warwick, everything reminded me of Dad. We passed the Friendly's Ice Cream Parlor where I split my eye open and Dad scooped me up and ran me across the street to the house. I had blood gushing down my face, and he dodged car after car, trying to get me home and bandaged up. He patched me up with a butterfly bandage placed horizontally along my caterpillar eyebrows. He said it was cheaper that way.

Each time the bandage was changed, my eyebrow hairs were pulled out. I didn't end up needing stitches, and the bandages lasted twice as long as they would have if we'd used two bandages vertically. Spending a month with no left eyebrow was a small price to pay. Dad said it made me tough.

We drove past the convenience store near our old house where Dad used to buy us whistle pops or WWF ice cream bars on his way back from the liquor store. Amanda and I talked about our trips to Rocky Point Amusement Park when we were kids. If we went on the carousel, Dad would be waiting for us with surprise Mickey Mouse balloons.

My mind returned to the dresser, standing clean and tall, adorned with shining reminders of his children and all that he'd lost, and reminding me of what I should've known all along.

10

LARRAIN

We viewed my father's body the Thursday after he died. I remember it was a Thursday because I'd bitched about how long it had taken for the medical examiner's office to release his body and about how we needed to get this over with so he could be at peace. Of *course,* he had to go and die on a long weekend; he had to be difficult right up until the end.

We didn't have a funeral, or a memorial service, or so much as a kind word, or even a funny anecdote. I told the funeral home to clean him up, slick his hair back because Amanda said he would've hated it if they parted it, put a suit on him, and lay him out in the chapel so we could see for ourselves that he was really gone. We might not have believed it otherwise.

My sister and I held two viewings that day – one early in the morning, against my father's wishes, so his mother, my grandmother, Larrain, could pay her respects, and one later in the morning so my aunt and uncles wouldn't have to see Larrain. They'd all been through enough.

I reminded Larrain several times that week about the day

and time of the viewing. Once when I'd gone to the house to get Dad's things, a second time when I took my sister there, and then twice more over the phone. I repeated myself to her, knowing that she probably wouldn't retain any new information over her rambling about my grandfather holding a reception at the Legion for my father and not inviting her.

"He's holding a coalition for your father at the Legion. Can you believe that?"

"Yeah, I know, Grandma. Thursday. 8 a.m. Don't forget, okay?"

"Raymond hated his father, and now he's doing that for him."

"Grandma, Thursday at 8. Make sure you're ready when I come pick you up."

"And he doesn't invite me. I'm his *mother*. I ought to go up there and hock up the biggest clam in my throat and spit in his face —"

"Amanda and I will be here Thursday morning to pick you up, Grandma."

When we arrived on Thursday morning, she wasn't ready.

"Where'd Cappy go?" I asked. Cappy was my father's crack-head friend who'd been at the house with Larrain every day since Dad died.

"Oh, he left. I'm not gonna go. I didn't know what time it was."

"Yes, you did, Grandma. I told you."

"Oh, well I'm not gonna go." I almost left her then. I didn't think she deserved to be there. I was certain that if she dropped dead in front of me right then and there, I wouldn't have cared. But Dad would have.

"Grandma, you need to get dressed."

"I'm not going."

"Grandma, they're taking him away to be cremated right after this. If you don't see him now, you won't get another chance. This is it."

"Come on. I'll help you get dressed," my sister offered. Larrain reached for Amanda's hand and they walked to her bedroom.

A few minutes later, Larrain emerged hand-in-hand with my sister, wearing a burgundy velvet dress and small black heels. Amanda escorted her down the icy front steps while I started the car.

We didn't speak much on the drive to the funeral home. When we arrived, I walked ahead and opened the doors leading to the chapel. We'd originally planned on waiting by the door while Larrain paid her respects.

"I can't let her go in alone," Amanda said, and we followed Larrain down the aisle, toward the front of the chapel.

I saw a familiar forehead peeking out from inside a white cardboard casket. No one told me it would be cardboard, and I had this idea that they had a loaner casket for circumstances like these. I walked toward the front of the chapel, half angry about the cardboard casket, and half hopeful that the person in it wasn't Dad after all. As I got closer, I saw the familiar nose, the one that was just like my sister's. I saw the full lips, also like my sister's, curled into the familiar smirk that belonged to Dad and Dad alone. It was him. I was certain now.

I didn't kneel or pay my respects. This was just a dress rehearsal for the late morning viewing to come. Whatever I planned to do or say, whatever tears I planned to shed, wouldn't be done in Larrain's presence. I stood back as Amanda helped Larrain up to the casket. She walked towards Dad's head. Surely, she'd put on some noisy, obnoxious display like she did the day he died, screaming, "My Raymond! Raymond, oh no!

My Raymond!" loudly, as if to drown out the names she used to call him along with the memories of abuse and lifelong manipulation.

Every day since his death had been about her. She was mad that the medical examiner wouldn't tell her what happened. She was upset about the Legion. She was pissed about the brand-new cooler she'd just spent money on that went missing after Dad took it out on a bender the week before he died. She was mad that her Raymond would leave her when she couldn't live without him.

But there was no display. Her round, four-foot-nine frame stood by his coffin, almost up on her toes, as she gently ran her pudgy fingers through his short brown hair and whimpered. I waited for her performance, but nothing came other than a quiet, "My baby, my baby," every so often as she kissed his forehead. I looked on as she cradled his head in her hands and cried. I felt the corner of my right eye twitch as it fought the urge to cry. I came fully prepared to have to rein in her crazy so she could say goodbye to Dad. What I got instead was a woman who'd just lost her child, and I finally understood why there's no word in the English language to describe parents who've lost their children.

When Larrain was finished, my sister helped her out the door, across the driveway, and into the car. I walked ahead as Amanda helped her walk over patches of ice, and I started the car.

"He looked great. They did a beautiful job," I said.

"Are his brothers coming?" Larrain asked.

"They're coming later, Grandma."

"Oh, good. Tell them I'm very sorry for their loss. I know they blame me."

I felt my eye twitch again.

When we arrived back at the house, Amanda helped Larrain out of her clothes and into some pajamas. "Would you like some lunch?" Amanda offered.

"No, I'm good."

"Do you want some wine?" I asked. I knew what she wanted.

"Yeah, some wine would be good."

I went into the kitchen and filled a red Solo cup to the brim with some Franzia boxed red wine. I handed it to Larrain, and she thanked me.

"Do you need anything else?" I asked, though I had no intention of doing much else for her.

"Are you sure you don't want something to eat?" Amanda asked.

"No, I think I'm good."

"Do you want the TV on?" I asked.

"No, I'm good." She sat back in her brown leather chair and took a swig from her red cup.

"You have my number, so let me know if you need anything, okay?" I said.

Amanda and I left as Larrain sat in her living room alone, drinking wine from a plastic cup at ten o'clock in the morning. As I started the car, I leaned over to my sister, who was staring back at the house. I held out my hand.

"Congratulations, we never have to deal with her again."

Amanda's gaze remained fixed on the house, and I began to back the car out of the driveway.

"Dad would hate that she's alone right now," she said.

"We've done enough."

"He'd hate that she's alone."

"I know. Should we go back?"

We sat at the stop sign leading out to the main road, staring at each other. I waited for any signal from her to tell me to turn around. I'd turn around if she wanted me to.

"Mom and Chris are at Sunnyside. Let's meet them for breakfast," she said.

11

THE SAME ROOM

Mom, Amanda, and I were all wearing red, Dad's favorite color. My husband Chris was wearing his black, pin-striped suit that he always looked so handsome in.

"How was it?" Mom asked.

"It was fine," Amanda replied.

"Yeah. No drama. I was proud of her," I declared. I didn't tell Mom that there were a few moments where I felt sorry for Larrain. Most mothers would've been proud that their child showed compassion to someone who probably didn't deserve it, but Mom wasn't most mothers.

"We went in with her. I couldn't let her go in alone," Amanda said. Upon hearing that we'd already seen Dad, my mother studied our faces like she was looking for something, but I wasn't sure what.

"He looked handsome. They made him look ten years younger. Beautiful job," I said. It was the third time I'd mentioned it that day, as if there was something comforting in a younger-looking dead person.

"He was smirking, Mom. I don't think they can pose them

that way," I continued, though I didn't know what joy I was trying to find in him dying at 44 with a smile on his face.

"Are you sure you don't want Chris in there with you?" Amanda asked me.

"I'm sure."

"And you're okay with that?" she asked Chris.

"I'm here for whatever she needs," Chris said, putting his hand over mine.

"He never met Dad. Dad doesn't need to meet his son-in-law that way," I snapped.

"I'm just saying that if Josh were here, I'd bring him in with me," she went on.

"And that would be really fucking disrespectful."

"Okay, girls. That's enough," Mom said, as she paid the bill. Amanda glared at me as Chris squeezed my hand and led me to the car.

When we arrived at the funeral home, we waited in the lobby for my uncles and my aunt to arrive. I wondered what it would be like to have all of these people in the same room together, since Dad didn't have a relationship with any of them, and none had spoken to each other in years, save for my Uncle David and my father's half-sister, Jeanine. Three estranged siblings, an ex-wife, and two daughters made one hell of a guest list.

My father's youngest brother, Kevin, was the first to arrive. He wore an expensive black suit and a silver crucifix around his neck. He clutched a black, leather-bound bible. He quickly albeit awkwardly greeted us before finding a bench in the corner where he sat alone, staring at the ground, and fiddling with his bible. My father's younger brother David was the next to arrive with his wife, Heather, and my Aunt Jeanine. He'd come straight from work, wearing a red polo shirt, jeans, and a baseball cap that covered his grey hair. Kevin stood to greet him and they shook hands and exchanged pleasantries, not like brothers, but not like enemies either, which I saw as a win. As Kevin went back to sit on the bench, I hugged my Uncle David and my Aunt Jeanine. My sister and I thanked him for wearing red, even if it was by accident. I talked about how handsome and young Dad looked, and I cracked jokes because I didn't realize how hard it would be to see my uncle that sad.

As we laughed about how Dad would have surely bragged about how sexy he looked in his suit, Aunt Jeanine wiped tears from her eyes.

"Oh god, that's too funny. You're so strong. I don't know how you do it," she said.

"Stop it," I replied as I noticed Uncle Kevin, still sitting alone, still fiddling with his bible. His showing up at Larrain's house the day I arrived in Warwick had softened me toward him – the way he was disgusted by how Dad lived, like he knew he deserved so much more; the way he endured being called an "asshole," and "douchebag," by Larrain and the crack-head so I could secure my Dad's belongings; and the way he helped Chris and me with our Red Cross message so Chris could get emergency leave. Whatever had happened in the lifetime before didn't matter; he showed up. And that was something. Something was better than nothing. I made my way out of the group and sat beside him.

"How are you doing, Uncle?" He didn't look up at me, and Amanda and Mom slowly made their way over.

"I don't know what he was looking for. I just wish I knew what he was looking for," he said.

None of us did. I looked at Uncle Kevin and saw the pain on his face and the frustration that I knew nagged at all of us and the shock that this was really happening because we always thought we'd have more time to make this all right.

"He just loved you girls so much," he said with tears in his eyes and with a facial expression that reminded me of my father. Instinctively, I looked away, and I saw my Uncle David, smiling, not out of happiness, but because it was better than the alternative. Watching those two men feel the loss of their brother made it hard to stand tall. It made the lump in my throat harder to swallow. It made the rush of tears harder to fight.

I had invited my grandfather, but he declined. "I don't want to see him like that," he said, looking down at the table, smoking his cigarette, and looking like the spitting image of my father if he were twenty years older.

"I hope you know how much he loved you, Grampa." Grampa looked at me with tears in his eyes and nodded. I wondered if he believed me. When it came to Dad and all his demons, there was a lot I didn't know, but I did know one thing; Dad loved his father. People who get mad about shitty relationships are usually only mad because they want them to be better, and that always comes from a place of love. I knew that better than anyone.

My father's older brother, Stephen, was serving a prison sentence after beating up my father and stabbing their neighbor. My father didn't press charges, though I'd urged him to. "He's still my brother," he said, and, thanks to my father's loyalty, Stephen was serving a much shorter sentence behind bars as we gathered to say goodbye. No one would have invited him anyway. He called me later that day. "I just want you to know that I loved my brother and I'm gonna do some things differently when I get out of here." I pictured Dad with the black eye and the bruise on his chest from Uncle Stephen.

"God bless you, Alicia," Stephen said just before the prison pay-phone cut out. Just as well. I didn't have anything to say to him.

When everyone had arrived, I ushered them toward the

door. Chris stood by a chair at the entrance. "You good out here?" I asked.

"I'll be right here if you need me," he said.

"Larrain might show up. Or someone trying to pull some shit."

"I'll make sure they don't. I'll be right here."

I walked ahead of the crowd, and as David's wife, Heather, went to sit with Chris, I put my hand on her shoulder and ushered her in, even though I had told her that it would be just immediate family. Later that night, she asked me what changed my mind.

"You're the only one who's done nothing but tell nice stories about him since I got here," I said.

We entered the chapel one by one. "They put him in *cardboard*?" my mother asked, sounding as horrified as I felt the first time I saw it.

"Yeah, and you know he's up there thinking, 'That's right, I can even make this box look sexy,'" I said, and everyone laughed one last time.

We took our seats in the chapel. Mom, Amanda, and I went up first, and I studied Dad's face: his smirk, the one he always had when he wore like a badge of honor when he was particularly pleased with himself, the goatee that he always thought was so cool, his crew cut and the swirly bald spot on the top of his head that was from an electrical injury when he was a kid. I tried to ignore the site of his half-shaved head and the stitches left from the autopsy. I saw his long brown eyelashes, the ones I'd inherited, the ones that left people asking me where I bought my eyelashes before I'd proudly declare, "They're *mine*."

When we sat back down, I held Mom's hand as she and Amanda cried together. Everyone went up and kneeled by the cardboard casket. First, Uncle David and Heather. Then

Auntie Jeanine. Then Uncle Kevin. Then everyone was seated. We sat for what seemed like hours, but was probably closer to ten minutes. It was quiet, save for everyone's weeping. I thought about how I couldn't remember the last time all of these people were in the same room. I tried to remember what we'd all been fighting about, but I was drawing a blank. I thought about what a train wreck we were as a family, and nearly laughed when it occurred to me that someone actually needed to die for all of us to be civil.

We sat there, with our fucked-up histories and stories, kicking ourselves in the ass for our stubbornness, for not trying harder to get him the help he needed, for committing the sin of thinking that there'd always be more time. I listened to their sobs, each one unique, each laced with its own special brand of guilt and grief, each one hoping that he knew how much he was loved by all of us.

"Okay, you know he's probably starting to get pissed off now. We should start wrapping it up," I said. With tears in his eyes, Uncle Kevin nodded in agreement.

"I'll go say goodbye first," Mom said. She knelt by his head and ran her fingers through his hair. She kissed him long, but gently. "Goodbye, My Love," she whispered before walking out.

I watched my sister kneel down and hold his hand one last time as she cried over him. "I love you, Dad," she said, as I felt the lump in my throat rise again.

One by one, everyone passed me. I saw the looks on all of their faces as they exited the chapel, knowing that this was the last time they would ever see my father's face. I saw my Uncle David cry for the first time in my life, and I felt my stomach knot up as he sobbed over his older brother, stroking his hair and kissing his forehead. Everyone marched past me, until I was the last one in the chapel.

I walked up to the casket and took Dad's giant hands in mine once more. I examined the smirk again, feeling strangely comforted by the idea that he saw the bright light and went sprinting towards it, like whatever he'd always been looking for, he'd finally found. I smiled as I looked over him one last time.

"Okay. I know that went on a little longer than you would've liked, but you'll get over it. You got them all in one room getting along. How about that? Don't worry about anything. Just get some rest now. I've got this. I'll take care of everything. I promise."

I clutched his hands in mine, memorizing the weight of them and what they felt like. I remembered every inch of his face: The goatee, the perfect nose and pouty lips that Amanda inherited, his olive skin, his thick brown hair. Everything.

I went to leave and, not knowing what else to do before we parted, I leaned down and sang part of the chorus of "Hakuna Matata," from *The Lion King*. I thought of how we spent our last day together, seeing that movie again in the same theatre he'd first taken us to see it when we were kids. Now, looking down at his lifeless face, I finally knew what Dad's worry-free days looked like. I rested my forehead against his, fighting back the tears that had been trying to come out since this all began. One made its way down my cheek and onto his. I wiped our faces dry and kissed his cheek.

"Bye, Dad. I love you."

I walked out through the double doors where Chris waited for me.

"Are you okay?" he asked as he hugged me.

"I'm fine. What's on your suit?" I pointed to a white smear on his shoulder.

"Heather was crying and needed a hug."

"Thank you."

"I love you."

"I love you, too."

* * *

I stood in the lobby as I was pulled in different directions. First, Amanda and I needed to sign the cremation order. Next, we needed to draft his obituary. "Make sure you include that he passed away peacefully in his sleep. That's important. He'd be proud of that," I said. After some back and forth with the obituary, I excused myself to use the ladies' room.

I checked to make sure the stalls were empty. I locked myself in the biggest one and rested my back against the door and slid down to the floor as my knees buckled under me. I punched the stall as hard as I could as I hyperventilated. "Fucking cardboard casket," I gasped as my fist hit the wall one last time, and I started to catch my breath.

I wiped away a few stray tears that had managed to escape. I used the toilet to pull myself up off the floor. I flattened out the wrinkles in my dress and straightened my blazer. I washed my hands and fixed my makeup and smoothed out my ponytail. I grasped the door, counted to three, and joined my family back in the lobby.

I saw my uncles talking to each other. Mom, Heather, and Auntie Jeanine were there, too, and Amanda was talking about her recent engagement. I looked at these people in the same room getting along, and I wondered if it would ever happen again. I wondered if the novelty of Dad's death would wear off, and soon our newfound family harmony would disappear like a post-9/11 American flag bumper sticker. I thought that maybe, just maybe, his death could bring us together, like a real family; if we could come together, if we could do the impossible, then maybe we might all be able to sleep at night.

I closed my eyes and smiled. *Please let this last forever.*

* * *

I called Uncle David on Christmas morning. Just as I'd promised, I'd done better about keeping in touch with the family.

"Merry Christmas, Kid. Did you get anything good?" he asked.

"I got a sweet hoodie, some cash, and a Patriots Snuggie from Chris's grandparents. It's pretty awesome," I said.

"That's nice, except for the Patriots Snuggie. Green Bay all the way," he laughed. He told me how he was enjoying his day off, because he never takes days off. He talked about the three pounds of bacon he made for breakfast. I heard what I thought was my Uncle Kevin in the background.

"Here, you wanna talk to Grampa? He's right here," he said as he handed the phone to my grandfather. I wished him a Merry Christmas as he passed the phone to my great Aunt Sis and she handed it to my Aunt Jeanine, who then handed it to Heather.

"Wow, so everyone's there?" I asked.

"Yeah, Leash. This is the best Christmas I've had in years," she said, her voice trembling.

"I wish he was there to see it."

"Me, too. Hang on. I'm gonna put you on speaker. Kevin's making a toast."

I listened as Uncle Kevin asked everyone to raise their glasses.

"To Raymond. We miss you. We love you. Wish you were here, brother."

"To Raymond," they said, and I could hear their glasses clinking.

"To Dad," I shouted into the receiver, with tears in my eyes, "Merry Christmas, everyone. I love you guys."

* * *

Raymond R. DeLory, Jr., 44, of Namquid Drive passed away peacefully in his sleep, Saturday, February 16, 2013. Born in Warwick, he was the son of Raymond R. DeLory, Sr. and Larrain (Reccko) DeLory. Raymond was employed as a carpenter for the carpenter's union. Besides his parents, he is survived by two daughters, Alicia Barksdale and Amanda DeLory; three brothers, Stephen DeLory, David DeLory and Kevin DeLory; one sister, Jeanine Wolf; and the mother of his children, love of his life, Kimberly Imondi.

12

THE GARDEN

I spend the morning running around Savannah, going to three different nurseries looking for the right rose bush. I don't want knock-outs because that would be too on-the-nose. At the third nursery, I settle on a baby rose bush with yellow roses. It's pouring outside by the time I get home, but I still go outside and start pulling weeds.

"Sweetie, just wait until it stops raining," Chris says. I ignore him as I put on my rain boots and my gardening gloves.

The rain pours down on me as I frantically pull the over-grown weeds along the back side of my house. There is a lot of work to be done because I've never been much for yard work aside from mowing the lawn, and even then, I mow everything, even the tulips that bloom along the side of the house. As I wipe away the raindrops in my eyelashes, I glance to my right at the chairs on my covered patio. That's where we were a month before when I found out I was pregnant. I paced back and forth while Chris tried to calm me down, "You'll be a great mom, Sweetie."

"No, I won't. I'm crazy and impatient and I'm gonna screw it up."

"No, you won't. Everything's gonna be fine." He repeated this to me as many times as it took for me to believe it, and then we called our parents to tell them we were pregnant.

There is one weed that looks more like a small tree that has grown just taller than I am. I start digging at the root and pulling. There will be no weeds in my garden. My garden needs to be perfect and clean. I cut it down close to the ground, then pull and hack at the stump. Chris has to come out and help me. He pulls and hacks and digs and cuts it down as far as he can until he finally gives up, and we decide to bury what's left. I toss the pieces we cut into the pile of weeds by my fence line. When the area is clear, we walk back into the house.

Chris sits at the table with the test strips he uses to make sure the water in the fish tank is suitable for our betta fish, Jeff Gordon. Jeff Gordon normally resides in his tank in our dining room, right next to my Dad's framed velvet painting of Jeff Gordon's race car. The day before, we noticed that Jeff Gordon was acting weird, and Chris has spent the last day or so trying to figure out what's wrong.

"Sweetie," I say, "we've had that fish for almost three years. I think he's just old."

"No, I think it was the spring water I put in there," he says, looking distraught and guilty.

"I doubt it. Even if it did, it was an accident." Chris toils away with his test strips, repeatedly testing the water pH while Jeff Gordon sits in a smaller bowl of water.

"The weeding's all done. Do you want to come out and help me bury it?" Chris doesn't look up from the strips.

"Yeah. I'll come out with you."

"Okay, you grab the rose bush and I'll go get the thing." Chris takes the potted yellow rose bush outside. I go into my bathroom and open my makeup drawer. A quart-sized Ziploc bag is waiting for me right where I left it the day before. Inside is a small sack, no bigger than the palm of my hand, and floating inside of it is the vague grey silhouette of our baby.

At the doctor's office the day before, they said that the baby had probably stopped growing after seven weeks. I lay flat on the exam table while the ultrasound tech searched for a heartbeat. I was scared because I'd noticed some spotting when I'd gone in for my urine test.

"Don't worry, Sweetie. I'm sure everything's fine," Chris said.

Click.

Zoom.

Click. Click.

Zoom.

Click.

Click.

Click.

"And there's the yolk sac," the tech said. And just before I could let out a sigh of relief, she finished, "...but there's no heartbeat. I'm sorry."

When I meet Chris outside, he's already started digging the hole. "Did you get it?" he asks.

"Right here," I say as I hold up the bag as if it's some frozen broccoli. When the hole is deep enough, I start opening the Ziploc.

"Wait. Should we say a few words?" Chris asks.

"You can if you want to." I continue opening the Ziploc and tip it over into the hole. As I gently wiggle the bag, ushering the embryo into the ground, Chris speaks.

"We love you, Bun. We had a lot of fun with you while it lasted."

"I'm sorry I couldn't make a better home for you," I say as I begin to sprinkle dirt over the moist little bubble. I remove the rose bush from the pot and place it over Bun. For the brief time I was pregnant, we lovingly referred to our baby as Bun Barksdale.

As I pat down the last of the dirt around the bush, I take a pink rose from the other bush my neighbor planted years before in memory of my father, and place it under the new rosebush. The bush is surrounded by nothing but dirt. Chris and I stand over the little grave in silence. I don't know what to say to him, and he doesn't know what to say to me.

"This looks like shit," I say.

"You did a good job weeding."

"No kid of mine is staying like this. Let's go get some mulch."

Everything after my ultrasound was a bit of a blur. The only question I remember asking was, "When can I drink again?" I remember going down to the hospital pharmacy to fill a prescription for Cytotec, which would induce contractions. I remember the lady behind the counter hugging me before I left. I remember the nurse practitioner inserting the medication inside me, and me joking as some of it fell out onto the exam table.

"Man, I can't keep anything up there." I remember being aggravated when that frigid hag didn't so much as crack a smile.

I remember the elevator ride down to the lobby and Chris waiting for me to say something. "Can we go get waffles?" I asked. He nodded and we went out to breakfast and talked about everything but the doctor's appointment.

Hours later, I keeled over in pain, sitting on my toilet with a mixing bowl on my lap, sweating and puking, and yelling at Chris to stop watching me because if he stayed much longer, my vagina would be ruined for him forever. Against my wishes, he stayed, holding my hand while I sat on the toilet and bled and shit and vomited. When I was tired, he walked me to our bed and held me, until I got up again, and felt something fall into my pants. When I raced to the bathroom, he helped me fish the sac out of my pants.

"I think we should get this white picket fence stuff," I say, piling little white wooden pickets into our cart.

"What about this brick?"

"Let's do that, too." We gather mulch and fence and bricks into the car, and as Chris starts the engine, he looks over at me.

"Are you okay?"

"I'm fine."

"You don't want to talk about it?"

"You were there. We don't need to talk about it."

"I thought you'd at least want to talk to me," he says, looking more hurt by me than I've ever seen him. All I can think about is Dad crying over his stillborn son, and me seething every time he did.

"Oh, my god, that was so long ago," I'd say.

"He needs to get over it already. He had kids eventually," I said, not knowing any better.

I think about all the things I've said about Dad's sadness about his son, and I'm sorry. I'm sorrier than I've ever been about anything. I want to tell Chris I'm sorry, but I don't know why. I just know I want to. I know he wants to help me, but I don't have the heart to tell him that he can't. So, I say nothing. Sometimes nothing is best. He waits for me to say something, and when I don't, he puts the car in drive, and we head home.

Since the nurse practitioner has failed to mention that I shouldn't be doing any heavy lifting, I help Chris haul the bricks out back. We work well into the night, spreading mulch and nailing fencing and brick into the ground with a rubber mallet. We place solar lights throughout the little garden so we'll be able to see the rose bush, even at night.

When we are almost finished, I remember that Chris's grandmother has given me two lady bugs made out of bowling balls and I go into the garage to find them. I pass Jeff Gordon's water bowl on my way inside, and notice that he is on his side and he's stopped moving. I try to nudge him with my finger, but he remains still. He's gone.

I grab the ladybugs from the garage and meet Chris outside. We place the ladybugs on opposite ends of the garden.

"That looks great," he says.

"Yeah. Looks like we hired someone." We stand outside and admire our work.

"Hey Sweetie, I think Jeff Gordon's gone," I whisper.

"What?"

"Jeff Gordon. He's gone."

Chris brushes past me and goes inside to the little water bowl. "C'mon buddy," he says as he nudges his lifeless blue and green body. He hangs his head.

"It's my fault. I used the wrong water and I killed him."

"No, you didn't. He was old."

"The pH got all fucked up and I killed him. Fuck. I'm sorry." I try to tell him that it isn't his fault, but he won't believe me.

"Let's bury him next to Bun, okay?"

Chris picks up Jeff Gordon's bowl and I go outside and start digging a hole, just a few inches from the yellow roses. I pour Jeff Gordon out into his tiny grave, and as I do, Chris begins to cry. The only other time I saw him cry was the day my father died. I'd just found out Dad was gone, and I paced back and forth on our patio, wide-eyed and in shock. "He's dead. He died. He just — he's dead," I gasped. Chris froze in front of me, scanning me, searching for some sign of what he needed to do. He'd never met Dad and only knew him through stories. He started sobbing.

"I'm so sorry, Alicia," he said as he tried to embrace me.

"No. No. Fuck you. Stop it. Get it together. I'm not doing this right now," I yelled, swatting him away from me as I pulled out my phone and began to dial my mother's phone number.

"He was such a good little fish, you know? He had a personality and it's like he always knew when it was time to eat because I'd come home from work and he'd swim around all excited," Chris says, weeping. I can feel the tears welling up in my eyes as I shovel dirt over the fish.

"He really was. He was a fish with personality. We love you, Jeff Gordon," I say as I wipe tears from my eyes and pat the dirt down.

It starts to drizzle again, and Chris and I stand outside in the dark, holding hands and weeping over the graves of our babies.

13

ASHES

W e trudged along the overcast coastline of Conimicut Point, peering through the frozen rain, looking for the perfect spot to pour Dad's ashes. As the frigid wind blew, I wrapped Dad's leather jacket tighter around my shoulders, clasping its broken zipper shut with my hands. The salty air was cold and heavy, and the ocean was barely visible through the fog. The beach was quiet and deserted; the only sounds coming from the gentle rumble of crashing waves and the squawking of seagulls in the distance. February in Rhode Island wasn't an ideal time to spread someone's ashes — another item on the list of inconveniences I associated with his sudden, tragic death.

We walked around trying to find the right spot among the rocks. The shoreline was littered with slick, brown boulders riddled with green and white barnacles. I couldn't distinguish one set of rocks from the other, but Mom knew what she was looking for; she wanted that one spot on Conimicut Point where they'd been photographed together decades before. I remembered that photo: Mom, with her feathered brown bob that I always said looked like a mullet, snuggled up on Dad's lap with his denim jacket draped over her shoulders, both of them peaceful and quietly in love. Dad sat on the rocks while one of his giant hands blanketed Mom's left thigh, and the other cupped her lower back. His baby-faced grin peeked out from her chest. They sat blissfully on the sun-kissed grey and white boulders overlooking the ocean, unaware of what was to come.

My eyelashes morphed into tiny icicles from the freezing rain, and I saw a flock of baby seagulls hobbling along the sand. I'd spent the first eleven years of my life living in Rhode Island and I'd seen countless seagulls, but never once had I seen a baby. I forgot about the task at hand and marveled at the cuteness of the tiny chicks. So, *this* is what they look like before they grow up to chase little children down the beach, squealing and squawking at them to give up their clam cakes or ice cream cones under the threat of death by pecking. But *these* little guys were adorable.

My sister, Amanda, pointed at the orderly line of chicks waddling their way through the sand. "Look at the babies!" We marveled at the baby birds and, for a moment, we weren't two women laying our 44-year-old father to rest.

"Oh, wow, look at them. I've never seen that before," Mom said.

"That's got to be a good sign," I said, hoping that in the vault of good omens, a giant group of seagull chicks signaled some sort of peace to come. Silly, perhaps. But a flock of feathery cuteness couldn't mean anything ominous. I was sure of it.

"There. Right there." Mom pointed to a cluster of rocks to the right of where the gulls were walking. "That's the spot." She sounded relieved, as if she were worried that this particular part of the beach had somehow gotten up and moved somewhere nicer. Connecticut or Massachusetts, perhaps — there's a lot less litter there. Either coast would be ideal for a nice piece of beach looking to settle down.

We ventured toward the boulders, trying to figure out the best place to spread the ashes. I climbed the rubble and started to slip and slide. I clung to the burgundy tote bag that held Dad's urn as my flats and their lack of tread provided me with no traction on the rocks. Mom and Amanda stood by, laughing and heckling.

"Careful, Lee. Don't fall. Water's cold this time of year."

From their position in the sand, they could see an opening in the rocks that led into the ocean. In between their giggles, they motioned for me to pour the ashes there.

I pulled the urn from the maroon bag, and was surprised to find that it was a black plastic box, plastered with shiny gold stickers advertising the crematorium. What a horrifying display of opportunistic advertising. *I'm already sold on your services, but I'll be sure to keep you guys in mind the next time someone drops dead.*

This would never have happened if I'd gotten him a proper urn and not selected the cheapest package the funeral home had to offer. I already owed them nearly $2000, but I didn't realize that a little bit of dignity cost extra. Two grand, and all Dad got was a viewing in a cardboard casket, then his remains cremated and crammed in a cheap black plastic box covered in stickers so he could be used for free marketing. He deserved better from life, better from me.

"Seriously?" I shouted as I frantically peeled the stickers off. "Who *does* that?"

Mom and Amanda snickered at me as I tried and failed to get rid of the stickers. As they came off in small pieces, the adhesive making an even bigger mess than if I'd just left them alone, I found myself wishing I'd listened to my parents when they repeatedly told me to stop biting my nails.

I tried to open the thick plastic lid on the urn. It wouldn't budge. Amanda and I took turns trying to pry it off. Mom hovered nearby, giving instructions and micromanaging as she often did, which only served to annoy us. It was like moving day all over again, when Amanda and I were hauling a dresser as Mom followed behind, doing what she referred to as "supervising," almost chanting the words, "Don't drop it," just in case we felt the sudden urge to carelessly dump it somewhere between the stairs and the moving truck and move on to whatever reckless or careless activity we would concoct in the split-second Mom wasn't telling us what to do. Considering the sensitive nature of our current circumstances and the task at hand, I ultimately decided not to meet her suggestions with an emphatic, "No shit."

"Maybe I should push it?" I asked. Amanda shrugged approval. I pushed the lid down, and after a hard thrust, the lid collapsed inside, revealing the clear plastic bag filled with what was left of my father.

"You're squishing him," Amanda shouted. We cackled with delight.

"I can't do *anything* right." I struggled to flip the lid back up. Our continuing laughter helped me catch my breath after seeing the ashes. The sight of that bag of white powder knocked the wind out of me, and I was glad my own nervous chuckling could conceal the gasps that would have followed the horror of seeing Dad reduced to an ivory mass of dust and ashed bone.

"How do you get this fucking thing open?" I screamed.

"Just...I don't know..." Mom was laughing too hard. I finally got the lid off of the urn and pulled out the clear, cellophane bag of ashes, which was fastened with a gold twisty tie.

"A twisty tie. Really? Sealed for freshness, I guess," I joked.

Mom and Amanda grinned and snickered again, and I felt grateful. I was glad I could make them smile during this ordeal. Dad was still with us for the next few minutes. Sure, as a pile of dust — an entire human life cut short by addiction and by one bad decision after another, now reduced to a bag of ash — but with us nonetheless. Soon, he'd be washed away with the tide and gone forever. There was nothing funny about that, but it didn't stop me from trying to find the punchline.

I held the bag in the air, almost proud, as if I'd conquered the lid and the ashes were my trophy. It reminded me of Dad and the way he clutched a bronze medal I'd won when I was ten. I placed third in a softball pitching competition, and I was disgusted. A bronze medal was for third place and third place was just the second-place loser, but Dad was *proud*. I couldn't understand how a man could be so proud of his kid taking the bronze, but he brought it to the construction site to show off at work. He'd come home, covered in drywall joint compound and sawdust, telling me how impressed everyone was with my medal and how he was going to mount it on the hood of his truck. I should have been moved. I should have felt overwhelmingly, unconditionally, and completely loved the way I do now anytime I picture him holding my medal, beaming with pride as he wielded my bronze medal when I knew he deserved the gold.

"Do I just...dump it?" I asked, looking to Amanda and Mom for guidance. I'd never done this before, but surely there was a more ceremonious way to dump a bag of human ashes into the ocean.

"Let's say a prayer first," Mom said. Without a snarky retort or mention of how much Dad would have hated this, we joined hands and prayed. Mom said something about God taking Dad into his embrace in Jesus's name or whatever, and then it was time. I unwound the gold twisty tie and climbed back onto the rocks, slipping and sliding as the rain continued to pour. When I gained footing, I poured the ashes into the ocean. I did it slowly and as gracefully as my balance would allow, until the bag was empty and the remains left a white mound in the water. I climbed down from the rocks and stood with Mom and Amanda to wait for the ashes to drift out into the ocean.

I pointed to the water near the rocks. "Mom, there's a big pile of Dad just stuck over there."

"Just wait. The tide will take it out." We stood in silence. The mound just sat there, getting no closer to drifting out to sea. This was no way for someone to be sent off. I stomped over to the rocks and climbed back up, but the rain was falling harder, and it was even more slippery than before.

"We had *one* job," I said as the freshly poured pile of Dad's ashes sat there in a big, wet heap of mud, failing to be carried out to sea.

Mom looked toward the overcast horizon. "The tide will come." But the tide wasn't coming, and all that was left of my father was a stagnant blob of white powder, trapped between a wall of rocks along the beach.

I fought the slickness of the rocks and crouched to stick my hand into the freezing water to try to wave Dad's ashes farther out. I slipped a few times, and after a few close calls and more laughter from Mom and Amanda, I threw a tantrum. "Oh Jesus, if I slip and fall into a pile of Dad, it's going to ruin my whole fucking day."

"Careful, Lee," Mom and Amanda shouted through laughter. I waved and swatted at the water, careful to not touch the ashes, willing the mound to disperse and move with the current, but it remained intact near the rocks.

I slipped and slid my way back to Mom and Amanda. "Meh, the tide will come in at some point," I conceded and I trudged over between my mother and sister, my ankles and pant legs soaked. Amanda went to the slippery rocks and climbed up with little struggle. She leaned near the mound and braced herself, dipped her hand into it, as if taking him by the hand one last time, and waved the ashes into the opening in the rocks that led out to the wide, gray ocean. I loved her more in that moment than I ever had.

She waved her hand with her familiar calm and gentle air, and in the silence, I heard her start to sing. It was quiet at first but grew louder.

Hakuna Matata.

I joined in, and we sang the song together, louder and jazzier, and Mom looked on, smiling at her children sending off their father in the best way they knew how. The song came to a close, and we stood together once more. With tears in our eyes, we watched the tide roll in and out, taking his ashes farther and farther away from us. Mom pulled us closer to her as she whispered, "He's free. He's *finally* free."

14

COUNSELING

We've been seeing Dr. Sue for a few months. I don't remember exactly why we started seeing her, and since I don't remember it, it was probably because of something stupid. I usually remember the serious things, and I make sure everyone else does too. Stupid brought us here; important kept us here.

We go every other Wednesday afternoon. We're almost always a few minutes late. I either bitch at Chris about his driving — he's always following too closely, and I complain that I'd rather be a few minutes late than dead — or I won't bitch at all, and he asks me why I'm not saying anything, if something is wrong, and we end up bitching at each other anyway.

We get here and schedule our next appointment while we wait for Dr. Sue to come get us. Chris comments on the neat and orderly magazine table in the waiting area.

"Mmm, you like that, huh?" I say.

"It pleases me," he grins.

"Weirdo," I laugh.

As we giggle quietly in the lobby, Dr. Sue, a petite woman

in her seventies who wears brightly colored palazzos and has the soothing demeanor of a yoga instructor, greets us by handing us both a cup of water, a gesture that Chris always appreciates. She leads us up a creaky wooden stairwell to her office. Chris sits closest to the door, and I sit closest to the tissues.

After our sessions, Dr. Sue leads us back down the creaky staircase, and I beeline to the restroom, whether I have to go or not. I meet Chris outside as he waits for me beneath the live oaks. He opens his arms to me, waiting for me to hug him, regardless of how the session went. I always hug him back and we tell each other, "I love you." We walk to the car, hand-in-hand, and we drive up the street to Blowin' Smoke Cantina for some tacos to complete our Wednesday ritual.

I sit in Dr. Sue's office three months into our routine, staring at the window behind her, as she asks how everything is going.

"How's your VA counseling going, Chris?" she asks.

"I'm still doing it."

"That's good. That's progress. Do you think he's making progress?" she asks me.

"He's trying," I say, still staring out the window.

"You don't sound too impressed."

"He's in the thick of it. It's gonna get worse before it gets better."

"Exposure therapy is a difficult road," she says. Chris and I nod. He hates his VA counseling and is only doing it because I said I'd only go to marriage counseling with him if he sees a counselor on his own.

When he isn't working, he sits on the couch, watching YouTube videos and stuffing his face with sweets.

"Babe, what's wrong?" I ask him.

"I don't know."

"Are you depressed?"

"Yeah, maybe."

"About what?"

"I don't know."

"How can you be depressed for no reason?"

"I don't know."

Dr. Sue examines our faces. It drives me crazy when she's silent. She knows if she waits long enough, I'll fill the silence.

"He's still depressed," I say.

"Is that true, Chris? Are you still depressed?"

"I guess so," he says.

"He doesn't know why," I sneer, "He's depressed for no reason."

Chris stares at the floor. He won't look at me. I wait for him to look at me. I wait for him to look sad or ashamed or indignant. I wait for any reaction. Something. Something is better than nothing.

Dr. Sue sits silently. I hear the clock ticking. I see Chris's left eye twitch.

"I hear a lot of anger coming from you," she says.

I roll my eyes and shrug.

"His depression makes you angry?"

"No. Being depressed for no reason makes me angry. He's alive. He has a good job. I bust my ass trying to be a good wife to him. And here we are, almost five fucking years later, and we're still dealing with this shit and I've got a husband who can't get off the couch and hates his life and wants nothing to do with me."

Chris's eye twitches again and his leg starts shaking. Dr. Sue looks at him and he smiles, something he does when he's uncomfortable. Sometimes it's endearing, and sometimes I want to smack the grin right off his face.

"I started making to-do lists on my phone," he says.

"That's a start. He's showing up," she says. I roll my eyes.

"You don't think it's a start?" she asks me.

"I don't know what else I can do to make him happy. Why the fuck are you so sad?" I fold my arms and clench my fists.

"Alicia, we can only control our own happiness," she says.

"Yeah, I know."

"Do you?"

"I keep trying to tell her," Chris says.

"Tell her what?"

"It's not her. I'll get over it. She can't fix it. She's always trying to fix me," he says, through clenched teeth.

"Oh, fuck you. You 'don't need fixing.' Remember?" I snap.

"That's *really* helpful," he says.

Dr. Sue stops us. She makes us practice our deep breathing exercise and our mantra. Inhale. *Ohm aim hreem shreem.* Exhale. *Ohm aim hreem shreem.* She makes us do this when we start to get too loud. It's supposed to regulate our prana energy or something. Neither one of us really knows what that means; we just know it calms us down.

"Alicia, are you trying to fix Chris?" she asks me.

"No."

"She talks about me like I'm dead," he says.

I smirk.

"I just don't see why I can't just be in a rut," he goes on.

"Is that what you think it is? A rut?" Dr. Sue asks.

"Yeah. I just get this way sometimes. I'll be fine. It just happens," he says.

"Out of nowhere? For no reason?" I ask.

"There's probably a reason, even if he doesn't realize what it is yet. And that's okay," Dr. Sue answers.

"This is bullshit," I say as I throw my hands up in the air.

"What's bullshit?" Dr. Sue asks.

"You didn't die. No one you knew died. We have a good

life. You have a good job, and I'm really fucking good to you. What the fuck do you have to be so sad about?" I scream.

"Alicia, I told you I'm just depressed. I don't know why. I'm just in a funk. I'll get over it. I told you I *am* happy to be alive. What else do you want?" Chris pleas.

"I want you to fucking act like it. It was five years ago. Get the fuck over it!" I shout as I pound my fist on the table between us.

"Alicia, it's just a funk —"

"Act like a fucking person who's happy to be alive. Stop wallowing. People wallow and they fade away and they give up and —" I choke on the last part of the sentence. My face flushed. My heart is racing. My fist is still on top of the table. I can hear the medical examiner's voice in my head: *Ethanol, Gabapentin, Neurontin, and Quetiapine. Accidental overdose.*

* * *

"My father never took pills," I said.

"Do you know if he had a doctor or someone prescribing these?" the medical examiner asked, though it was probably a secretary or something. I doubt it was the actual examiner.

"My father didn't take pills. He knew better."

"I'm sorry for your loss."

"But my father didn't take pills. How much did he take? Did he do it on purpose?"

"We can't make that determination. It's been ruled an accidental overdose."

"But how much? Did he take the normal dosage or...did he take a lot? My father never took pills."

"He took a higher dosage than recommended."

"So, he could've done it on purpose? Can you tell —"

"It's been ruled an accidental overdose. I'm so sorry."

* * *

"Alicia," Dr. Sue says.

I'm frozen, still trying to catch my breath.

"Alicia. Alicia, can you look at me?" she asks calmly.

I unclench my fist and turn towards Dr. Sue. I tuck my hands between my knees.

"Alicia. Which people wallow and fade away?"

I'm silent.

She looks at me, waiting.

"Daddy issues," Chris mumbles. We laugh.

* * *

I douse my face with cold water in the restroom and pat it dry. I walk down the blue-carpeted hallway and exit through the front door. Chris is standing on the sidewalk beneath the shade of the Spanish moss hanging from the mighty live oaks of downtown Savannah. He turns to me, his arms outstretched.

"Want a hug?" I hug him.

"I love you," I whisper in his ear.

"I love you too. Tacos?"

"Tacos."

15

THE SNORKEL

Many of my childhood summer weekends were spent at my great Aunt Connie's house. My parents would bring their collection of coins, secured in an old, empty tub of butter, and they'd gamble all night long while playing High Low Jack with Dad's cousins on the screened-in porch. I would spend the day swimming in the in-ground pool, going down the slide and being careful to never cross the rope that led from the shallow end to the deep end. The night usually ended in Auntie Connie's den, where Amanda and I would pass out on the carpet after watching Disney movies all evening, unless I watched *All Dogs Go to Heaven* or *The Land Before Time*. Then the night ended with my parents comforting me while I sobbed over the death of Charlie the German Shepherd or Little Foot's mother.

I spent much of my pool time alone, while my parents watched me from the porch. Amanda didn't spend as much time out there as I did, and could always be found sitting on Dad's knee while he played cards, cutely asking Dad every few minutes if his hand was any good. If someone was eating something, Amanda would go from lap to lap, asking for bites of food, and no one could say no to her because she was so adorable. I was protected by swimmies or an inflatable life jacket that was always one size too small and tied too tight. My mother called out to me every few minutes to make sure I kept them on. I had a tendency of taking them off when they became too uncomfortable.

I was six or seven when I almost drowned. I'd flirted with the deep end by grabbing onto the dividing rope and letting my feet float over. "Get off the rope or get out of the pool!" Dad or Mom would shout from the porch. I just wanted to feel the water without having the swimmies on my arms. I wiggled each one off when no one was watching, and floated around the shallow end. The cool water felt good against the red marks I had on my tiny biceps from where the swimmies squeezed me.

I climbed out of the pool when I had to pee and scurried in towards the house. The concrete by the pool was slippery, and as I ran, I slipped and fell into the deep end. The water went up my nose on impact, and I started choking on the pool water. I thrashed my arms and legs as hard as I could, but my body continued to sink below the surface. I gagged as I screamed, "Help me!" under the water. I saw the tall, blurry figure of my father standing over me. He didn't pull me out right away, perhaps to teach me a lesson.

He reached his arm into the water, grabbed me by the front of my bathing suit and pulled me out of the water. I gasped and coughed and threw up water all over the cement.

"See what happens?" Dad shouted. "You got a belly full of water, don't you?" he scolded.

"Raymond, you tell her she'd better not be drinking all my pool water!" Auntie Connie shouted from the porch. The other adults laughed as my mother screamed at me from outside the pool fence.

"Where are your swimmies, Alicia?"

"She's fine," Dad said.

I lost my pool privileges for the remainder of the weekend.

The next weekend, Dad reminded me on the drive to Connie's that I was not to go in the pool because I couldn't behave like a big girl. I went straight to the den and watched movies by myself while Amanda stayed with Mom and Dad on the porch. A while later, Dad came to get me. "Come with me," he said.

He led me out to the swimming pool. I stood next to him while he sipped from his Coors. After a few swigs, he shoved me into the pool. I thrashed and gagged once again for a few moments until he pulled me out and held me so I was eye-level with him. "Daddy's gonna teach you how to swim."

He spent the rest of the day with me, teaching me how to dog paddle. I picked it up quickly. By the end of our lesson, he held my waist while I dog paddled into the deep end. Each time he'd let go, I'd dip into the water a little and get water up my nose. He kept holding and letting go until I could dog paddle on my own.

That evening, Dad brought me inside and told my mother, "She doesn't need swimmies anymore. She's a mermaid now."

"No swimmies, and no deep end without an adult, okay?" Mom said.

The next few weekends, Dad spent more time in the pool with me, teaching me how to backstroke and do cannonballs. I don't remember where Amanda was during all of this. I can't place her anywhere in those memories. I imagine wherever she was, she probably wasn't happy that she wasn't on Dad's knee.

By the end of summer, Dad surprised me with a blue snorkel and matching goggles. "We still gotta work on the water up your nose kid, but you're a swimmer now," he said. I was excited to try out my present at the pool. I paddled just under the surface, in awe that I could see and breathe underwater. I don't remember why I left the pool for a few minutes that day. I don't remember what Amanda was doing there. The only other thing I remember from that day is that I'd set down my snorkel for some reason, and when I came back, Amanda was standing there with it in her hand.

"That's *my* snorkel." I said, holding my hand out.

I don't remember her saying anything back. She grinned, raised her hand as high as she could, and threw my snorkel onto the pavement, breaking it in two.

I stared in horror at my shattered snorkel, lying lifeless on the pavement. I immediately regretted parading my snorkel around, waving it in Amanda's face, talking about how Dad bought a snorkel just for me. I didn't know it was so easy to push a toddler to the edge. "My snorkel!" I screamed as I lunged toward my sister, shoving her into a lounge chair. My father pulled us apart. "What happened?"

"She broke my snorkel." Amanda smiled at me as I said this. When Dad looked at her, her smile disappeared.

"Did you break her snorkel?" Dad asked her. Amanda started crying.

"Alright," he said, "it was an accident and you don't put your hands on your sister."

"But —"

"But nothing. You keep your hands to yourself. Come on, Panda," he said as he carried my fake-sobbing sister back into the house, leaving me alone to seethe over the fragments of my prized snorkel.

No one seemed to care about my snorkel. Amanda never got in trouble for it. Nobody even seems to remember it now. Eventually, I got another snorkel, but it wasn't the same. I'd been mourning the loss of my old one for weeks, and summer was ending. Dad came home one Saturday morning with a plastic yellow Cost Plus bag in his hand.

"I got a surprise for you, Kid." He pulled out a package with the same blue goggles and snorkel he'd given me weeks before.

"My snorkel!" I was so excited and I held it to my chest. I promised myself I would cherish it and take such good care of it and I'd never take my eyes off of it.

"Panda, Daddy got you something too," he said. Amanda's face lit up as she giddily stood next to me and held out her hands. Dad pulled another package from the bag, this time containing a green set of goggles and a snorkel.

"Green's my favorite color!" she squealed as she jumped up and down.

"She can't even swim," I said.

I still think of my dear snorkel from time to time. I asked my mother about it and not only did she not remember it, but she vehemently denied that my nearly drowning ever happened. Amanda didn't remember it either.

"You know, the snorkel Dad got me after he taught me to swim. You grabbed it and broke it on the cement by Auntie Connie's pool," I reminded her.

"No. I don't remember that at all. But that sounds like something I would do," Amanda laughed.

"Do you know why you might have done that?"

"Probably because he was spending time with you and ignoring me."

"Yeah, but he liked you better."

"No, he didn't. He talked about you all the time."

"You spent more time with him."

"Yeah. But he talked about you all the time. And he was so happy when he did see you. Like I was chopped liver," she laughed.

"He talked about you too. Said what a good daughter you were, visiting your father all the time. Made me feel like shit."

"Yeah, and you took charge of everything when he died. Now *that* made me feel like shit." We're both silent for a moment. I could hear my nephew cooing in the background. I didn't know what to say. I just knew I was sorry.

"All that fussing over his hair, and we find out he had a buzz cut," I joked. "I'm sorry. I'm sorry for all of it, Amanda."

"I know you are, Lee. I'm sorry I broke your snorkel."

16

AFGHANISTAN

It's September of 2016, which is almost a year after he got out of the Army, nearly four and a half years since he returned from Afghanistan, and five and a half since he saw combat.

We bought a house when we moved back to Savannah, GA, just one street over from his grandparents and the home he grew up in. The leaves haven't started to turn, because the humid South Georgia heat hasn't yet made way for the cooler autumn breeze. My house smells of pumpkin from the fall-scented candles I have burning in all the rooms. I zig and zag through my living room with a feather duster, cleaning and humming. I dust the picture frame that is mounted above our couch and contains photos of the people we used to be. I don't pause in front of them anymore or wonder where those people went. That was before, and here, in the after, I'm cranking up the volume of the music blaring through my headphones, clearing away the dust on the faces of the people I used to know, and I reassure myself that, deep down, they are still here somewhere, and I will make it here another day.

At my request, he's sitting on the small sofa in our spare bedroom, waiting for his virtual therapy session with the VA to begin. He had an appointment yesterday, but he moved it. "I'm too tired today," he said, but promised he'd do it the following morning. Talking to a computer screen once a week isn't ideal, but it's better than the once per month he got in the Army with their only solution being to adjust his meds. Now, he settles in on the beat-up tan loveseat, the first piece of furniture we ever bought, and he situates his laptop securely on his thighs. After he puts in his earbuds, he clutches a brown throw pillow, pulling it to the side of his torso, bracing for impact.

He locks himself in the spare room, and I do my best to keep the dogs quiet. I sing along to my music, and as I walk through the kitchen, I shake my head at the pile of empty donut hole boxes on the counter, waiting to be carried out to the recycling bin. They're his favorite comfort food, and it's been a rough week. There's a leaning tower made of four empty boxes of comfort monopolizing my counter. I demolish the tower, crushing the boxes one by one, and I carry the rubble outside to the bin. I stay on the other side of the house, so I don't overhear anything. I begged him for years to tell me what was eating him.

"I can handle it," I'd say.

"I don't want to bother you with all that shit," he said. And that's where it ended. I wouldn't understand anyway. After all these years, I'm starting to think that maybe I *can't* handle it, that maybe something that's held onto him for so long is too big for my civilian brain to comprehend. So, I don't ask questions and I don't try to understand anymore. I don't make him talk to me, and I've stopped talking to him about things because he's got enough on his plate. And I can't hate him for it, because he was a hero.

Heroes are exhausting.

"You don't have to talk to me, but you have to talk to someone," I said, telling him instead of asking, making it known that I'd given five years of my life to his ghost or shell, or whatever it was that he'd become, never knowing what it was that took him away; I wouldn't give him five more. I wouldn't spend more time being afraid to come home while he was sleeping during the days after his night shift, worried that he'd mistake me for an intruder. I'd sing as I walked through the door, humming loudly and deliberately as I disarmed our house alarm, hoping it would be enough to let him know it was me before he reached for his 9-mil in the nightstand. He said we'd be safer with weapons in the house, that he'd feel better if he knew he could protect me and the dogs if he needed to. The irony is not lost on me. I wouldn't spend another night afraid to fall asleep in his arms, wondering if he'd sleep through the night or wake up screaming or pulling my hair or swatting at an invisible something and accidentally hitting me.

I know I was kinder in the beginning. I'd stroke his hair and rub his back once he came to. "It's alright. You're home. You're home," I'd whisper as he caught his breath and went back to sleep.

Now, I sleep with three dogs between us and my back to him. I sleep with a knife on my nightstand, and I pretend that I'll be able to fight him off if it comes down to it.

"Shut the fuck up," I shout when he wakes up screaming.

"Sorry," he says, the words muffled by his sleep apnea mask.

I know whatever it is that's eating away at him has hardened me. I used to be kinder than this. Neither one of us is the person we used to be. "What are you thinking about?" I'd ask when I saw him drifting off. I used to wonder what it was that left him awake at night, screaming. I liked myself better then; he did too. I've given five years of my life to the shadow of someone I used to know, just hanging around, waiting for a glimpse of who he used to be, never knowing who or what or why this has happened. I've watched him be beaten down for years, but I don't know how much more time I can spend if I don't know what's hitting him.

Someday, a little more than a year from now, he'll hand me the recording from today's session, and he'll do it like it's nothing, because by then, this will all just be another chapter in his story, just another thing that happened to him in his life. But now, that day seems so far away, and I'm turning up the volume of my playlist so my headphones drown out the voice coming from behind the closed door at the end of our hallway.

He sits in front of his laptop with his earbuds in. "Can you hear me?" his counselor asks a bunch of times because the software — like most of the other VA resources — is slow and outdated.

"I can hear you."

She asks him about his stress levels lately. Anxiety in public is a three out of five. She asks him about thoughts of suicide.

"How does my answer impact my job?" he asks.

"What do you mean?"

"In the military, they told us not to answer that question."

"I have to report it if I think you're a danger to yourself or others. But a thought isn't necessarily an imminent danger to you."

"I mean, it's just a 'What if?" he says.

"How so?"

"Sometimes Alicia and I will be leaving the house, and I'll have my weapon with me and for a second, I just think, 'What if I just put it to my head and pull the trigger?'"

"And then what?"

"And then it goes away. I don't think about it beyond that."

"It's normal to have those thoughts."

"Or sometimes, I'll be in the car, and I'll think, 'What if I just lay on the gas and drive into a brick wall?'"

"And then?"

"And then it's over. I don't think about it again."

She tells him that these thoughts are normal, especially with his anxiety levels. She tells him she's not concerned, but to let her know if he needs help or the thoughts get worse. She asks him to rate his level out of five on the suicide question.

"One," he says. Old habits die hard.

He tells her about our trip to the grocery store the other day. Grocery shopping is the only time he leaves the house now. He talks about our trip to lunch that day. I hate going out to eat with him. He scans. He looks for a seat where his back can be to the wall. He gets anxious towards the end of the meal, rushing me out the door.

"We might as well eat at home," I sneer, "This isn't even fucking worth it." I know I used to be more understanding than this. I'm so tired.

He rates his anxiety during our day as a four out of five. She asks him more questions. She tallies his answers.

"Your anxiety is about the same, but given the work we're doing, that's not surprising."

"Okay."

"Your PTSD score went down slightly, so that's an improvement."

"Okay."

Before they dive into his imaginative exposure for the day, he asks, "Can we switch to bi-weekly sessions?"

"Why?"

"Because I fucking hate doing this. I'm drained from this shit."

"You feel drained because you're doing the work. It's going to get worse before it gets better."

"I hate this. No offense to you, but I'd rather be anywhere but here. Maybe switching to twice a month would make it better. Maybe that needs to happen."

"If you hate me a little, then I'm doing my job. I can take it. I know this sucks. But *this* is what needs to happen."

"Okay."

"Thank you for telling me that. And thank you for being here anyway."

He laughs. "Okay."

"The only way out of this is through it," she says, and he laughs again because this is something I've started saying a lot since my father died, and it's what I say to him when he tells me how much he hates his therapy.

She decides that they will start at the spot in his story that triggers him the most. She tells him to pay attention to his SUDS level throughout, which I've learned means "Subjective Units of Distress," and is basically just a way of saying how stressed out you are on a scale of zero to 100.

"Okay, Christopher. Close your eyes. Let's start when you see the first RPG," she says.

The first RPG. I see it coming towards me. It loses its propellant. It slows down a little bit, bounces off the ground. I duck into the vehicle. "RPG! RPG! RPG!" I brace for impact. I just remember a few seconds later, coming back to, and then getting back up into the turret and re-engaging.

"What's your SUDS?"

"40."

He's beyond "mild anxiety/distress, no interference with performance," but he's not quite at "moderate anxiety/distress, uncomfortable, but can continue to perform."

"Okay, let's go through it again. More detail this time. You're doing great.

I'm staring out over the turret through the sites of the 50-cal, firing into where I believe they're at, because I can see the dirt kicking up and the muzzle blast. So, I'm firing in there and then I can't really see exactly where it came from because it left that area so fast, but I see an RPG probably about 150-200 meters out in front of me. I see it coming towards the vehicle at a really fast pace. The end of it was oblong with a long, skinny end to it, and had the fins in the back, and it was just cutting through the air. At first, I couldn't really believe it, but once I saw what it was, I see it getting closer and closer, and I'm thinking, "Holy shit. This is real."

It's getting closer and then once I saw it kind of drop off, for a second I thought maybe it would explode and then it wouldn't be as much of a risk. But it didn't. It just kind of lost propellant, skimmed off the ground for a second, and then kept going. At that point, that sense of relief kind of fleeted away pretty quickly. And then I went back into "Oh shit" mode again. And that was when it got close enough that I released the 50-cal, ducked back into the vehicle — not all the way in, but just enough that I was out of the way of any shrapnel or something that would come up — and yelled down to Gritt, "RPG! RPG! RPG!" because that's what they train you to do. Yeah, that's what I said. And then we just kinda braced for impact. The vehicle shook a little bit. It just feels like vibrations to me. And then, I just know everything went black for what seemed like a few seconds.

Then, I got my bearings, got back up, got back into the turret and reassessed the situation. I scanned, looked around to see if I could see anything, maybe where it came from or something. At that point, I just kept firing in that general direction because I knew that's where it came from.

"What's your SUDS out of 100?"

"60."

Right between, "Moderate anxiety/distress, uncomfortable but can continue," and, "Quite anxious/distressed, interfering with performance."

"Okay. Again. More physical sensations this time. You're doing great."

It's hot. I'm sweaty. I can smell the gunpowder from the 50-cal. My wrist hurts. I can feel the shaking from the 50-cal as the firing block's going back and forth, back and forth. That just kinda rattles you each time it fires off. I'm trying to keep it steady as I look down the sites. I think my butt's getting kinda, not numb, but tingly because of how I'm sitting back. I've got a little flap of cloth that's kind of my seat for the turret. I just brace up against that, and I've got one foot propped up on one of the radio mounts, and that kind of gives me something to push off of to get a more stable platform to fire from.

I can't really hear much because of all the noise around me. All you can smell is the gunpowder. I see the landscape around me. I see the muzzle flash from that wadi that's in the distance. You can see a few little qalats nearby.

As I'm firing in that direction, I see an RPG that looks like it comes out of nowhere. I can't tell where it came from. I just know it's coming at me really quick. As it's coming at me, I don't have the reaction time to do much of anything. I was firing the weapon, looking straight ahead at my target, and then, my peripherals catch it coming at me. My adrenaline rush that I already had spiked even higher, if that's even possible. The most that I can feel from all this is just my anxiety, my fear, my excitement, and my adrenaline. It's all just the highest it's ever been. Once I saw the RPG coming at me, it was just like, almost a sense of enlightenment or something. It doesn't feel real.

"What's your SUDS level?"

"55."

"Again. This time, tell me what's going through your head as you see this thing coming at you."

It's coming at me.

I can't do too much.

It's coming at me.

It's coming at me.

I didn't have time to think. Just...you know, "Holy shit."

I see it drop and skip for a second and at that point, my body loosened up a little. I started to feel a little more relaxed. I thought maybe it was a dud. But then it picked back up and kept coming. And when it skipped off the ground, it was actually pretty close to the vehicle, maybe 50 meters out. It all seemed like slow motion.

It's coming at me. I'm tensed up again. It's kind of like getting into a car accident and you see the car coming at you. I tried to drop down just to get out of the way of the shrapnel and everything. I yelled, "RPG! RPG! RPG!" No unique feelings at this point except for the adrenaline. That's really it. There wasn't fear or anything. It was just kind of...I was there and that was it.

It's like you're on Cloud 9 — it's just completely different. You're just doing what you've been training your body to do. You're fighting back because you want to live. Whenever something like that happens, when it flies at you like that and you think you might die, and your adrenaline's spiked and everything else, you're not really thinking about anything else.

I didn't feel fear. I didn't feel anger. I was just existing.

All I know is I blacked out for what seemed like a few seconds. And after that, I just remember reassessing and re-engaging.

"What's your SUDS out of 100?"

"65." Just shy of, "Quite anxious/distressed, interfering with performance."

"What's the first thing you notice after blacking out?"

"Looking up at my gun."

"What are you feeling?"

Anger. And the adrenaline. And wanting to kill whoever did it. I feel it in my head and chest. I'm mad that I didn't see it sooner because then I would've been able to lay a few rounds in the dude that shot it. The guy actually had pretty good aim.

I ducked in for a second, told Gritt what was going on. And then, I remember it impacting and feeling the vibrations. It hit where I was at, maybe a little bit lower, so I got the brunt of the concussion.

I just remember blacking out for a few seconds. I don't know how long it was. They told us that the fire fight lasted like an hour, so there ain't no telling. Anyway, I come to, and I just start laying waste again.

"What are you thinking as you're laying waste?"

"Just killing everything I can."

"How much control do you feel at that point?"

"None."

"What's your SUDS out of 100?"

"60."

"How did that feel, reliving that event again?"

"Fine."

"Fine? That's some crazy shit. You almost died."

"You don't feel the almost dying part until hours after. During and even right after it's just...euphoric."

"But it was a close call. What would that have been like if it had killed you?"

"It would have been. That's about it."

"Did you think about how it would have affected your family?"

"No."

"No? Not at all?"

"No. I was worried that I might have killed civilians."

"Like innocent bystanders?"

"I worry about that sometimes. They shouldn't have been in the area, but still."

"That's something you think about?"

"Sometimes."

"So, was it really fine?"

"No. I guess not. It sucked. I fucking hate this."

* * *

She thanks him for showing up. She tells him to keep doing his homework, or they can't continue with his treatment. He commits to spending at least thirty minutes this week cleaning the garage. She makes him set a reminder on his phone so he won't forget. He packs up his laptop and sits on the sofa in silence, bracing himself for the rest of his day. Maybe he'll shower today. That's something. Something is better than nothing.

I hear the doorknob turn and his footsteps drag down the hallway. I make myself busy with loading the dishwasher. He brushes behind me and walks out into the garage. I hear him landing punches on the punching bag.

One two.

One two.

One two.

It stops after a few minutes. I hear him gasping, trying to catch his breath. The punches start again.

One two.

One two.

One two.

I scrub dried egg yolk from a plate. I hum to myself to drown out the punches and gasps.

The door leading to the kitchen from the garage opens. He stands behind me. His eyes are wide with dark circles under them. He's waiting for something. Always waiting. For what, I'm not sure because I'm a civilian. We're long past the days of guessing games. Time and time again, he tells me I wouldn't understand, so I've stopped trying to. If he needs something, he'll have to come out and say it. Marriage is rarely 50/50, but I can't do 90/10 anymore. Hell, I'd settle for 60/40. Fuck, maybe even 80/20. Something. Something is better than nothing.

I spoon some porridge into a bowl and start slicing strawberries.

"Breakfast?" I ask. His eyes lower to the floor. He takes the bowl and starts stirring. He looks up at me, softer this time.

"Will you sit in on my next one with me?"

ACKNOWLEDGMENTS

This book would not be possible without some truly amazing mentors: Eugenia Kim for her brutal but necessary crash course in writing, Carol Ann Davis for constantly reminding me to "stop trying to make everything *mean* something," and Bill Patrick for believing that I could turn this jumble into a coherent narrative, and then helping me do it. I'd also like to thank Sonya Huber for your guidance and friendship over the years—starting with my very first creative writing class—and for continuing to be someone I admire and strive to be as a writer, friend, and human being.

Thank you to the incredible Fairfield University MFA writing community for inspiring me in more ways than I can count. There's no way this book would exist without our little island.

Thank you to Lisa Kastner at Running Wild Press for giving this book a home, as well as Ben White for believing in this story and working so hard during our collaboration and multiple reads. You've both made this experience so incredible for me every step of the way.

A very special thank you to the Delory family for supporting me and this project, even when it was difficult or uncomfortable. Seeing you come together over these last few years and being able to immortalize it on the page has been one of the greatest joys of my life.

Thank you to my sister Amanda for filling in the gaps and dropping truth bombs when needed. You're the best person I know. Mom and Dad, as parents go, you were nothing short of miraculous. I love you both.

Finally, thank you to my husband Chris for trusting me with his story and being brave enough to share it.

BIOGRAPHY

Alicia Delory is a freelance writer, editor, and content strate-gist. She is a graduate of Georgia

Southern University and Fairfield University, where she received her MFA in Creative Writing.

She lives in Savannah, GA with her husband and daughter.

Past Titles

Running Wild Stories Anthology, Volume 4
Running Wild Novella Anthology, Volume 4

UPCOMING TITLES

Running Wild Stories Anthology, Volume 5
Running Wild Novella Anthology, Volume 5
Take Me With You by Vanessa Carlisle
Frontal Matter Two by Suzanne Samples
Blue Woman/Burning Woman by Lale Davidson
Antlers of Bone by Taylor Sowden
The Reremembered by Dwight L. Wilson
Mickey: Surviving Salvation by Robert Shafer

Running Wild Press publishes stories that cross genres with great stories and writing. Our team consists of:

Lisa Diane Kastner, Founder and Executive Editor
Barbara Lockwood, Editor
Peter A. Wright, Editor
Rebecca Dimyan, Editor
Benjamin White, Editor
Andrew DiPrinzio, Editor
Lisa Montagne, Director of Education

Learn more about us and our stories at www.runningwild-press.com

Loved this story and want more?
Follow us at www.runningwildpress.com,
www.facebook/runningwildpress,
on Twitter @lisadkastner @RunWildBooks